The Teacher of Generation Alpha

Nihal Yurtseven (ed.)

The Teacher of Generation Alpha

PETER LANG

Bibliographic Information published by the Deutsche Nationalbibliothek
The Deutsche Nationalbibliothek lists this publication in the Deutsche Nationalbibliografie; detailed bibliographic data is available online at http://dnb.d-nb.de.

Library of Congress Cataloging-in-Publication Data
A CIP catalog record for this book has been applied for at the Library of Congress.

"The thoughts and opinions expressed in the chapters in this book do not reflect the thoughts and opinions of the editor. All the opinions belong to the authors themselves, and in no way can they be accepted as the official opinions of neither Bahçeşehir University nor the editor of the book."

ISBN 978-3-631-80977-8 (Print)
E-ISBN 978-3-631-81885-5 (E-PDF)
E-ISBN 978-3-631-81886-2 (EPUB)
E-ISBN 978-3-631-81887-9 (MOBI)
DOI 10.3726/b16823

Peter Lang – Berlin · Bern · Bruxelles · New York · Oxford · Warszawa · Wien

This publication has been peer reviewed.

www.peterlang.com

Table of Contents

Editor's Preface

This book has been prepared in attempt to help teachers gain a multi-dimensional perspective about the current trends and approaches in teaching and managing their classrooms, which have started to welcome the youngest generation, called Alpha. As all educators know, each generation brings their distinct features to classrooms, which make teachers rethink their instructional practices and reorganize the learning environment to accommodate the needs of the students. Generation Alpha, similar to any previous generation, has its own traits that make it unique. Technology is obviously the most apparent contextual variable that distinguishes Generation Alpha from the other generations. They are called as the most tech-savvy group as they were born into a digital age in which smart phones, applications, and gadgets were widely used. Apart from technology, some other distinct features are worth examining to understand Generation Alpha. The book addresses all teachers, teaching any level or grade, regardless of their branch. The content of the book will help its readers gain perspective about thinking deeply on how to improve teaching.

The Teacher of Generation Alpha is organized in nine chapters. In Chapter 1, we provide a brief comparison of Generation Alpha with the previous generations, introduce their basic characteristics, and offer some recommendations about the ideal educational design. Chapter 2 examines the necessary skills teachers must obtain in order to understand Generation Alpha better and provides an understanding of the current context of Generation Alpha. Chapter 3 focuses on how to design the instruction by using a specific instructional design model, called UbD (Understanding by Design). Chapter 4 reflects on the recent theories and pedagogical implications about fostering student creativity in Alpha classrooms. It also summarizes approaches and methods for a creative classroom. Chapter 5 explains some differentiation strategies such as Cubing, RAFT, Menu, and Choice Boards that provide options for each student's learner profile and interest to handle individual differences. Chapter 6 offers self-management strategies, which enhance collaboration and innovation via changing norms and let students create and explore in Alpha classes. Chapter 7 focuses on measurement and evaluation methods for Generation Alpha and aims to enrich teachers' skills about integrating appropriate assessment procedures in the classroom. Chapter 8 aims to guide teachers on how to enhance the DQ digital citizenship abilities of Generation Alpha and ensure that they have these skills to satisfy the needs and challenges of the digital world. Finally, Chapter 9 focuses on providing data literacy skills for teachers so that they are able to meet the basic requirements of Generation Alpha and the environment they are born into. In short, we try to offer teachers recommendations and strategies in various fields throughout the book to address this new generation, called Generation Alpha.

Acknowledgments

I wish to express my deep appreciation to all the authors, who showed continuous encouragement, dedication, and interest in the publication of this book from the beginning. I feel indebted to teachers, administrators, students, and colleagues without whose feedback it would not have been possible to prepare this book. I would like to thank Prof. Dr. Tunç Bozbura, the Vice president of Bahçeşehir University for his great encouragement about preparing this publication. Lastly, I wish to thank Prof. Dr. Şirin Karadeniz, the President of Bahçeşehir University for her continued guidance and support and the peaceful environment she created to concentrate on preparing this publication.

Nihal Yurtseven, PhD
Bahçeşehir University, Istanbul, Turkey
October, 2019

Nihal Yurtseven and Şirin Karadeniz

An Overview of Generation Alpha

Abstract: Demographers and social scientists have named generations with different letters over the last 50 years, and it has always been a concern for educationalists to examine the characteristics of generations to fully understand their needs, preferences or tendencies in the learning environment. Starting with the silent generation, Baby Boomers, Generation X, Generation Y, and Generation Z have attracted the attention of a large environment. Considering the technological advances and scientific developments in years, we face the indisputable fact that each generation comes with its original and distinctive characteristics. Among the generations, Generation Alpha, known as "tech thumbs", has deserved the careful consideration of educationalists in recent years. This chapter focuses on Generation Alpha, which has been present since 2010 – the environment they are born into and the necessary teacher competencies that teachers need to prepare this generation for future. Tracking the characteristics of this special generation in detail will help the teachers gain a broad perspective of Generation Alpha and its most basic and commonly observed features.

Keywords: Generations, Generation Alpha, 21st-century skills, educational design

At a Glance: Generations

Defined as people in a society or family who are nearly the same age, the term "generation" connotes a group of people who share the environments of the same age, hence sharing similar worries, similar troubles, similar excitement, happiness and apprehensiveness. They represent a group of people united in a particular sense, display unprecedented levels of distinctness from the former ones and form a new sense and perception of life. Reis (2018), while mentioning the influence of key societal experiences such as dominant political, economic and cultural impacts, points out the prominence of molding of people in a certain period of time. These variables have the potential power for people to view the world differently from the older counterparts and give the majority of the cohort a new and unique meaning of life, thus paving the way for viewing the world from a different perspective. Their responses or reactions to specific subject matters and events also make them particular. This reveals the fact that every generation is exclusive and has unique characteristics in terms of lifestyles, values, priorities in life, thoughts and feelings (Williams & Page, 2011).

The fact that generations have profound impacts on different aspects of a society's culture cannot be underestimated. This influence may range from production and naturally consumption habits, art, politics, professional careers, family life to macroeconomic status and economic prospects of a country. This organic link between a particular generation and its priorities has unearthed the need to classify and label each of them. However, it should be noted that there might emerge some distinctive characteristics even among the members belonging to the same generation. Further, being exposed to different living conditions, having dissimilar personalities and uniqueness peculiar to mankind make the distinction among the boundaries of generations open to question. Nevertheless, partly due to the popularity of the subject matter along with its impact on social, economic and cultural agents, the concept of common characteristics of a generation has gained importance across the globe.

As is widely known, the current trend of globalization has spurred the increase in interaction through social media and internet, which causes any event happening somewhere in the world affect all the people and generations. These digital tools enhance the congregation of various generations from different parts of the world, as well. At the same time, the increasing trend of "glocalization" brings forward the idea of leaving the struggle to produce uniformity and experience the global locally through local lenses, which includes cultural distinctiveness, geographical and geopolitical diversity (Gobo, 2016). The underlying reason behind this viewpoint is that cultural values, the area being lived, and the critical position of a country strongly influence one's identification of the self and the potential production in collaboration with the stakeholders globally. McCrindle and Wolfinger (2011) point out that up to seven generations coexist in the home, workplace and community. This salient fact draws attention to the questions such as "What might be the possible effects of culture on generations?", "Can we identify every generation in the global sense?" or "Can we place individuals showing medium or high level of similarity at the same generational category?".

Apart from the inquiries that make the distinctions problematic, sociological phenomena should also be taken into consideration. Within this context, traditionally, one generation refers to the average time interval between births of parents and their children. This places the formation of a generation into 20–25 year interval. Although this definition has provided a good source of information to sociologists in the past, it requires rethinking. At the present time, a generation spans a period longer than what has happened so far since childbirth is postponed more than ever. As a natural consequence, the time interval between births of parents and their children has stretched from two decades to longer, which makes the sociological perspective significant all the more (McCrindle & Wolfinger, 2011; Parry & Urvin, 2010).

Although theoretical frame and empirical studies cannot precisely define the boundaries of generations for certain, an accepted case is the existence of distinctive cohorts that display dissimilar attitudes, beliefs, characteristics, expectations and priorities from the previous ones. We should not ignore that the fundamental structures of societies inevitably change due to economic, social, cultural, political and technological factors in the course of time. It seems visible that new generations are not so keen on understanding the building blocks upon which the previous generations and societies once constructed their lives. This generally results in somehow a gap which leads to conflicts among generations in terms of perceiving life itself. However, the culture and the value judgments that we own today is the product of former generations.

It is widely accepted that advancing or making progress in terms of social, economic and cultural life are solely possible through utilizing and benefitting from the experiences and the knowledge transferred from the past. As argued, common values and culture change somehow get a different form while transferring to a new generation. The fact that every generation comes into the world with the belief that it can change the course of events triggers taking several actions to make this change rapid and perpetual. What should frequently be highlighted is that the differences that mark the boundaries among generations display tendencies to change over time in accordance with the "zeitgeist" of a certain period.

All in all, in today's world, and probably for the first time in the recorded history, it is witnessed that members belonging to several generations are to live and share together. Increased life standards and life expectancy have allowed people to live longer, and this diversity in social life may result in ever-mounting conflicts and matters. Thus, it would be valuable in many respects to examine the generations and characteristics of the people who actively participate in social life and share in order to take especially educational actions and accommodate settings.

Generations before Alpha

Although the exact years are still disputable to make an accurate cut off among the labels, it is generally agreed that people born in 1945 and before are called as "Silent Generation"; people born between 1946 and 1964 are labelled as "Baby Boomers"; people born between 1965 and 1976 are called as "Generation X"; people born from 1977 to 1995 are termed as "Generation Y"; and people born between 1996 and 2010 are named as "Generation Z". The illustration can be seen in Fig. 1:

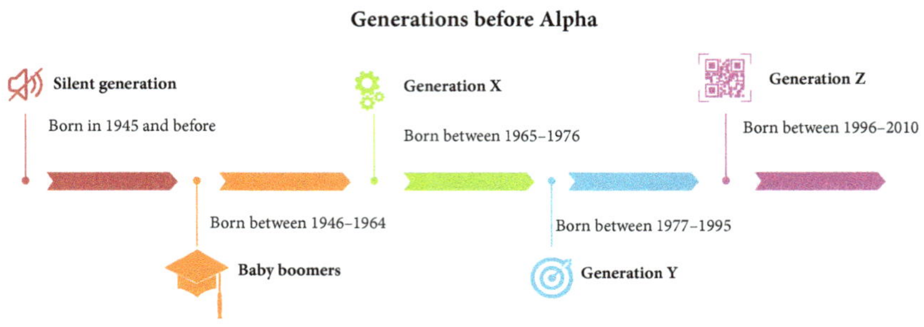

Fig. 1: Generations before Alpha

Silent Generation (Born in 1945 and before)

Also known as the traditionalists or matures, the silent generation is characterized as being conventional, fatalistic and disappointing. They never issue manifestos or carry out protests; instead, they are mostly withdrawn, cautious, and unadventurous. They either served or were the children of the soldiers in World War 2 (Henger & Henger, 2012). This generation witnessed some dramatic events as the passage of the Civil Rights Acts and 1960s' events that led to women's movements. As they witnessed World War 2 and faced the tragic Great Depression, they found themselves lucky enough to be employed (Lancaster & Stillman, 2002).

Baby Boomers (1946–1964)

This generation is the result of the dramatic increase in the birth rates after World War 2. Baby boomers is a quite competitive group in the sense that they set excessive goals and put so much effort to attain them (Underwood, 2007). They are dedicated, hardworking, and focused individuals whose values towards their work dominated their life. They liked working so much that they continued working even after the retirement age (Marston, 2007).

Generation X (1965–1976)

Compared to previous generations, Generation X has a more work-life balance. Although they hold strong beliefs in working hard, they care about their ongoing life outside of work and they try hard to improve it (Patota, Schwartz, & Schwartz, 2007). Having a happy family, feeling safe and maintaining their work-life balance are their major concerns. World events (as seen on TV), respected co-workers, and their friends' values and views shape their belief systems to a large extent (Gravett & Throckmorton, 2007).

Generation Y (1977–1995)

Known as Millenials, Generation Y is defined as an optimistic, social and self-esteemed group. Among all the previously mentioned generations, Generation Y is the most tech-savvy group that was born into an age of computers (Delcampo, Haggerty, Haney, & Knippel, 2011). Having a distinct profile, they have different perspectives on protecting the environment, respecting differences (about race, gender, ethnicity, etc.) and responding to challenge in the workplace (Gravett & Throckmorton, 2007). Although Generation Y has recently been unfairly stereotyped as being lazy, disloyal, selfish and spoiled, these imputations mostly remain as prejudice (PrincetonOne & Hobart, 2014).

Generation Z (1996–2010)

Also called as iGen and Centennials, Generation Z is identified as being kind, fair, compassionate, open-minded and humorous. Members of Generation Z have grown up in an increasingly diverse world in which borders have been removed and access to information have been so easy with the help of digitalization. This generation characterizes itself as being achievement-oriented, motivated through relationships, and focused in meaningful work (Seemiller & Grace, 2019). They are the first generation to have grown up in an entirely post-digital area. They never know a world without smartphones, mobile internet and social media. They are a multi-tasking group which can efficiently shift between work and play without getting distracted by the things going on in the background. They believe in family, diversity and equality (Fromm & Read, 2018). At school, they are more independent and self-taught compared to their parents or any other previous generation. Learning at their own pace and experimental learning opportunities are important in their learning process. (Seemiller & Grace, 2019).

Generation Alpha

Coined by the sociologist Mark McCrindle, the term "Generation Alpha" refers to children born from 2011 and up to 2025. Unlike the previous generations, Generation Alpha is the only generation that has wholly been born into 21st century (Tee, 2018). Although technology was a defining factor also for the preceding generations, Generation Alpha is obviously part of an unintended worldwide experiment as they are located in front of screens at a very early age. Distinctively, iPad was first introduced, Instagram was created and the term “app” entered into the lives of masses of people in 2010, almost the year they started being born (Williams, 2015).

Generation Alpha plays, interacts, and learns in different ways. Instead of being addressed as a homogenous community in classrooms, they attach great importance to making their own choices and expect their teachers to consider their individual needs. In addition, they value the integration of digital devices into their learning environment. Recent research has also found that they have better visual skills and cognitive abilities about hand-eye coordination because of playing digital games (Turk, 2017). Alpha children acquire knowledge much better by active participation in the learning process through experiments, cooperative learning, problem-solving activities or drama.

What Are the Common Traits of Generation Alpha?

To put it concisely, we can list the following as the most basic traits of this generation:

- They are eager to pose questions in the classroom. They are extrovert and fussy learners.
- They use the power of logical reasoning in the learning process. With this type of an approach, they exceed limits, they go beyond the information given to them and they clarify problems in their minds.
- They are good at making inferences, meaning that they use deductive thinking to conclude.
- They think strategically, which also expands their decision-making capacity.
- They operate their metacognition, which helps them plan themselves before taking action and monitor their learning process.
- They are creative, demonstrating originality and novelty in their products.
- They are tech-savvy; they grow up with the voice of Siri, Google Assistant and Alexa, and they are quite familiar with them. They value using a smartphone and are competent at doing it. YouTubers generally influence them. Compared to toys or pets, gadgets are much more important for them (Conklin, 2012; Eaton, 2018; Turk, 2017).

The common traits of Generation Alpha signal the existence of distinctive attitudes, characteristics, and expectations, compared to the previous generations. To get insight about how to prepare this generation for the future, it can be enlightening to examine how educational design should be made.

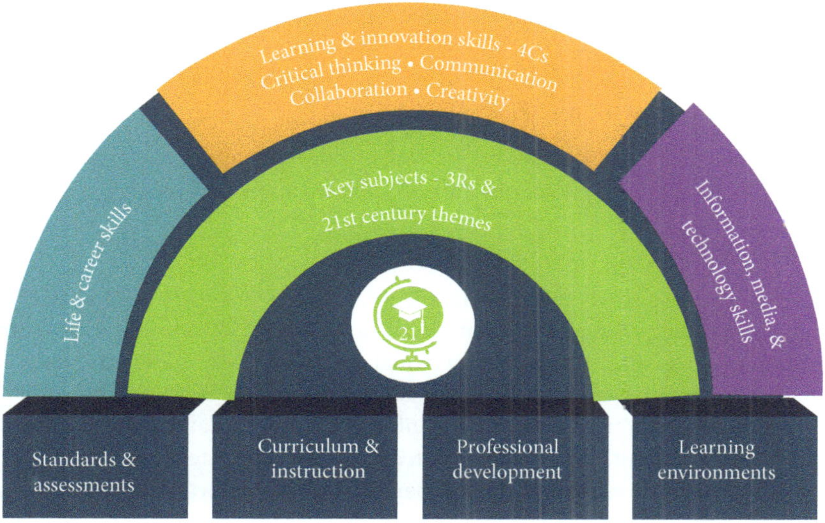

Fig. 2: 21st-Century Skills. Retrieved from: http://www.battelleforkids.org/networks/p21

Essential Skills to Cultivate for Generation Alpha

By the year 2030, Generation Alpha will reach the age of 20 and they will be the generation that will have worked for the longest period at the end of the 21st century. According to McCrindle and Wolfinger (2011), they will be the most job-fickle group, having approximately six different careers in their professional life. In order to define the exact requirements and necessities specific to this century, there have been numerous attempts, offering frameworks to conceptualize 21st-century skills. Among them, one of the most comprehensive and widely accepted is Partnership for 21st-Century Learning, based on the theoretical work of Trilling and Fadel (2009) as illustrated in Fig. 2:

Key Subjects – 3Rs and 21st-Century Themes

As part of the 21st-century skills, key subjects include English, reading or language arts, world languages, arts, mathematics, economics, science, geography, history, government and civics. In addition, the academic content at schools should be weaved into the 21st-century themes, presented as global awareness, financial, economic, business and entrepreneurial literacy, civic literacy, health literacy, and environmental literacy.

Learning and Innovation Skills

In this category, a learner's necessary skills to develop are represented in 4Cs, namely, critical thinking, communication, collaboration, and creativity.

Critical Thinking

Defined as a cognitive skill and intellectual disposition that is required for identifying, analyzing and evaluating arguments, critical thinking helps the learner discover and overcome personal prejudices, formulate reasons to support arguments, and make reasonable and rational decisions. A student who can effectively use the critical-thinking skill in the classroom can understand the arguments and beliefs of friends; can evaluate those arguments and beliefs; and develop and defend personal well-supported arguments and beliefs. An employer who can think critically in the workplace can think creatively; can solve problems; can gather and analyze information; can draw appropriate conclusions from data; and can communicate ideas effectively and creatively. Likewise, individuals who are good at critical thinking can avoid making irrational personal decisions; can help promote democratic processes; and can free themselves from unexamined assumptions and be self-directed throughout their life (Bassham, Irwin, Nardone, & Wallece, 2013). To be good at critical thinking, a student should do so many exercises similar to someone who practices playing tennis, golf or a musical instrument. Only in this way can a student be good at reasoning, make a balanced consideration of arguments, and use the appropriate techniques to evaluate claims. The strength in thinking critically prevents an individual from making ill-formed, knee-jerk and unjustifiable decisions throughout life (Moore & Parker, 2015). To promote critical thinking in the classroom, Beers (2011) recommends that students:

- be given enough time for a thoughtful consideration of a particular problem before starting to work with peers.
- be encouraged to put forward solutions and develop intrinsic motivation to trust their judgments.
- think deeply about the appropriateness of their decisions with the help of enlightening questions.
- use multiple perspectives to approach a problem.

- utilize collaborative problem-solving models in which they work as a group to solve a problem.

Communication

It is roughly defined as the exchange of information or the description of feelings that results in understanding. Individuals exhibiting good communication skills can skillfully present their thoughts and have significant edge on their peers (Delcampo et al., 2011). As is well known, the key to successful relationships rests on quality communication in all aspects of life (Gravett & Throckmorton, 2007). Individuals with quality communication skills can articulate thoughts and ideas effectively by using oral, written or nonverbal communication skills. These people listen effectively to interpret the meaning of content; they use communication as a tool for a variety of purposes including informing, persuading, teaching or motivating; and they can communicate with people in various settings (Battelle for Kids, 2019).

Collaboration

It is the situation of two or more people working together to complete a task or achieve an aim. In today's global world where borders have lost their significance and people can easily connect to each other across digital platforms; there is a strong focus on collaboration. Therefore, it is getting more and more essential to develop skills and competencies that are conducive to team work (Delcampo et al., 2011). Good collaborators demonstrate the ability to work effectively and respectfully with different teams. They can also make necessary compromises to achieve a common goal by showing enough flexibility and willingness. Most importantly, they share the responsibility and value the contribution of each team member (Battelle for Kids, 2019).

Creativity

It is the process of having genuine ideas that have value. Actually, current school systems around the world hinder the capacity of learners by inculcating them with a narrow view of intelligence and capability. Adopting a one-size-fits-all approach and neglecting the potential of students is a big threat to creativity. Children start school with a great imagination capacity, fertile minds, and enough courage to take risks. Underestimating the capacity of them and putting too much emphasis on tasks that do not foster creativity lead to drainage of the capacity for creativity (Robinson & Aronica, 2009). Though creativity is not a skill that can easily be taught, everybody has the capacity to create. Therefore, learning environments nourishing the uniqueness and creative expression of ideas are attached utmost importance in the 21st century (Kennedy, Latham, & Jacinto, 2016). To foster creativity in the classroom, Beers (2011) recommends teachers to make students:

- have enough knowledge about the content to generate ideas;
- understand the exact reason why a particular innovation is necessary;
- examine the situation by considering multiple perspectives;
- conduct further research in cases where there is still need for solid foundation of understanding;
- create solutions for the identified needs and justify their suggestions to others.

Information, Media, and Technology Skills

Three important facets are taken into consideration under this heading:

Information Literacy

It refers to two fundamental aspects of literacy: (1) Accessing and evaluating information, (2) Using and managing information. As part of information literacy, accessing information efficiently (time) and effectively (sources) as well as evaluating the accessed information critically is important. Moreover, it is crucial for an individual to use the information accurately, to manage the flow of information, and to apply an essential understanding of the ethical use of information and media (Battelle for Kids, 2019; Riedling, 2007).

Media and Technology Literacy

This literacy refers to analyzing media, creating media products and applying technology effectively. Individuals who can analyze media well can understand how, why and for what purposes media messages are constructed. They examine how individuals interpret media messages differently by taking into consideration values and beliefs, and they have an understanding of how media affect beliefs or behaviors. Creating media products requires individuals to understand and utilize appropriate media creation tools and ICT literacy. Applying technology effectively represents using technology as a tool to research, organize, evaluate, and communicate information. Individuals who can apply technology effectively can use digital technologies, communication tools and social networks to access, manage, and create information. They can also apply the ethical issues appropriately in the process (Battelle for Kids, 2019; Leaning, 2009).

Life and Career Skills

With this category, required skills for individuals in their life and career are defined. Five basic traits come to the surface as part of life and career skills:

Flexibility and Adaptability

Flexible individuals can incorporate feedback effectively; can deal with praise, setbacks, and criticism in a positive way; and can understand different viewpoints, negotiate with shareholders, and make a balanced consideration of diverse opinions. Similarly, adaptability refers to one's ability to adapt to different roles, job responsibilities, contexts, or work schedules. In real life and career, adaptability is important in the sense that it enables the employer to work effectively in a working environment where there is some ambiguity and priorities of individuals alter (Battelle for Kids, 2019). Teachers can address the following questions to students in the classroom to promote flexibility and adaptability:

- What changes have you encountered in your life so far?
- When it is not your choice, how do you react to change?
- Are you open-minded to others' opinions? Give an example (Beers, 2011).

Initiative and Self-Direction

This trait refers to one's capability to manage goals and time without direct instruction of outer figures and capacity for independent work. Having this trait helps an employer set goals with related success criteria, manage time accordingly, monitor personal progress, demonstrate the eagerness to advance skills, and show commitment to lifelong learning by reflecting critically on experiences (Battelle for Kids, 2019). The following questions can be motivating for students to consider taking initiatives:

- Do you take the initiative to manage your own learning?
- How do you manage your time?
- What are your personal goals about learning?
- How do you prioritize your tasks? (Beers, 2011).

Social and Cross-Cultural Skills

Having these skills expands an employer's capacity to interact with others effectively. They know when to listen and when to speak, and they act in a professional manner while doing it. Moreover, they can work effectively in diverse teams, especially in teams where there are cultural differences. In this kind of a working environment, they show an open-minded perspective to different ideas and values. They also leverage social and cultural differences to put forward new ideas and increase the innovation capacity of work (Battelle for Kids, 2019). Beers (2011) recommends using the following questions in the classroom to promote social and cross-cultural skills:

- What are the most important social skills to work with others?
- How does understanding another person's culture or background help you understand their point of view?
- Do you listen to others' opinions effectively without judging?

Productivity and Accountability

These traits are important contributors to an employer's capacity for managing projects and producing desired results. Such individuals in the workplace can prioritize, plan, and manage work to obtain intended results; can work positively and ethically; can participate actively by considering punctuality, present themselves in a professional and proper manner; can collaborate and cooperate effectively in teams; can be accountable for results (Battelle for Kids, 2019). To prepare students to be productive and accountable in work life, Beers (2011) recommends the use of the following questions in the classroom:

- Why is it important to set clear goals when conducting a project?
- How do you manage your time while you are doing a project?
- If you were an employer, what work habits would you want your employees to have?

Leadership and Responsibility

Having a leader identity requires an employer to guide and lead others by shouldering responsibility. Such leaders in the workplace use interpersonal and problem-solving skills to guide others toward a goal. In addition, they can leverage the strengths of others to accomplish a particular goal and they act responsibly by keeping the interests and tendencies of the group in mind (Battelle for Kids, 2019). To raise the awareness of students about leadership and responsibility, the following questions as an advice can be raised in the classrooms (Beers, 2011):

- What are the characteristics of a good leader?
- Give an example of a time when you were in the position of a leader. How can you describe your experience? What are the positive and negative sides?

To achieve the abovementioned skills, there should be a sound basement to ground the studies on. To accomplish this, Battelle for Kids (2019) identifies four basic support systems to ensure that every 21st-century learner gains the kinds of 21st-century experiences. These support systems can be named as standards and assessment, curriculum and instruction, professional development, and learning environments.

ISTE Standards for Students

Similar to the previously mentioned framework, ISTE standards for students refer to competencies that require students to be more autonomous, creative, and collaborative in essence. These competencies can be listed as: (1) Empowered Learner – leveraging technology to take an active role in choosing; (2) Digital Citizen – recognizing the rights, responsibilities, and opportunities of being in an interconnected digital world; (3) Knowledge Constructor – critically curating a variety of resources by using digital tools to construct knowledge; (4) Innovative Designer – using a variety of technologies in a design process to identify and solve problems; (5) Computational Thinker – developing and employing strategies to understand and solve problems; (6) Creative Communicator – communicating clearly and expressing oneself creatively by using appropriate tools and digital media; (7) Global Collaborator – using digital tools to broaden their perspectives and enriching their learning by collaborating with others locally and globally (https://www.iste.org/standards/for-students).

Skill Sets for the Future Workforce

As technology has impacted many areas related to human, the necessary skills for the future workforce have got its share from the recent developments. Jezard (2018) argues that three important skills will come to the forefront in the near future. These skills are (1) higher cognitive skills – skills that include advances literacy, statistical skills, and complex information processing; (2) social and emotional skills – skill that enhance communication, negotiation, the ability to become a lifelong learner and manage others to adapt; (3) technological skills – skills that include basic to advanced IT skills, data analysis, engineering, and research. These skills mostly refer to technology-related and non-cognitive soft skills. The Future of Jobs Report (World Economic Forum, 2018) underlines the importance of creating new opportunities for innovative partnerships of governments on a global scale and investing in a new type of education that will be beneficial to the prospective workforce of the 2030s.

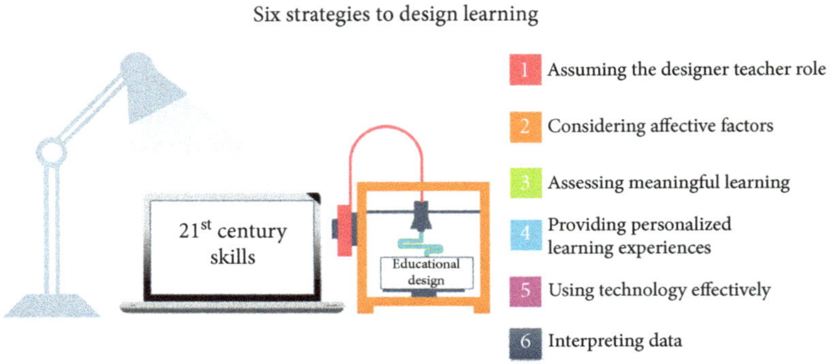

Fig. 3: Six Strategies to Design Learning

Educational Design for Generation Alpha

Lurking behind all the abovementioned facts, generational differences and the required skills for the 21st century are the questions about how to design learning. How can teachers make their classes welcoming for all students? What standards do they need to take into consideration while planning? Can they ensure the conformity of all learners in the learning environment? As can be examined in Fig. 3, the niceties of educational design signals the consideration of six critical elements in the designing process.

Six Strategies to Design Learning.

1. Assuming the "designer teacher" role

Ongoing emphasis on the necessity of teachers taking their own initiatives about planning the instruction and reviewing the curriculum has shifted the paradigm about teaching (Carl, 2009; Wiggins & McTighe, 2007). The new expectations from teaching require teachers to demystify the process of learning by adopting a multidimensional way of thinking. More pointedly, the designer teacher role helps teachers to tailor their instruction, make it more understanding-based instead of being coverage-based, and refine their teaching practices to become more student-oriented. In this process, it is important to set more tangible and pertinent goals, define the exact desired acquisitions, connect them with correct assessment tools, and propose a clear path of learning experiences. Making matters worse is regarding the components of instructional design as separate units though they should be patterned by nature. And yet, the rubber meets the road with the designer teacher role.

2. Considering affective factors

For learning to occur in the most effective way possible, laying a sound affective basis as well as considering cognitive processes holds great importance. In its simplest form, affective factors can be conceptualized as the learner's motivation, attitude, anxiety, self-efficacy beliefs, emotions, and feelings. Although cognitive activation is a frequently mentioned component in the learning process and holds great importance, disregarding the affective aspect of human beings can be hindrance for learning. In addition, concepts such as self-regulation and metacognition should be taken into account as they also have strong influence on learning, thought, affect, motivation, and action (Bandura, 1991; Zimmerman, 2000). The thoughtful consideration of these variables will make the learning atmosphere more attractive.

3. Assessing meaningful learning

Providing meaningful feedback and contributing to students' progress while continuing evaluative activities is one of the most important responsibilities of teachers. This responsibility leads teachers to set aside some personal obligations about checking whether students know every piece of information shared in the classroom. While shifting the focus from checking meaningful learning, this point of view also imposes a heavy burden on teachers. Instead of needlessly heightening the stress by treating reference books as the ultimate goal to be reached by the students, teachers' focusing on assessing meaningful learning and the possibility of students' transferring it to another context can be much more admissible (Wiggins & McTighe, 2007). In essence, educators need to become more assessment literate and professional practices regarding assessment and evaluation have witnessed a recognizable change in the last few decades (Chelimsky, 1997; Stiggins, 1995). To adapt to this change easily, answering the following questions can be helpful for teachers:

- Should testing and evaluation be limited to classroom?
- How can teachers put formative assessment into practice more effectively?
- Can educators evaluate student achievement in a holistic manner by examining the entire school life and students' social-emotional development as well? To do this, can they use technology-assisted systems instead of ranking exams that are summative in genre?

4. Providing personalized learning experiences

Because of globalization, easy access to information, and the emergence of gadgets addressing diverse interests, it is impossible to generalize people's preferences or put them in a single mold. Similarly, it is merely impossible for a teacher to treat students as if they are all alike. As we know, students learn more effectively when they are specially taken into consideration. In crafting the instruction, teachers need to do more than this to provide personalized learning experiences. There is an ill-structured belief that personalization accounts for individual learning. This is, in fact, a misleading assumption and creates great ambiguities. Providing personalized learning experiences connotes the differentiation of the instruction by regarding students' varying readiness and interest levels as well as learning styles. To accomplish this, the learning process, the content, or the product to be created at the end of learning item can be differentiated (Tomlinson, 2014; Tomlinson & McTighe, 2006). With this approach, the classrooms can be structured to make students become more proactive, involved, and expressive in their needs instead of a unitary approach to teaching.

5. Using technology effectively

It has been proved that technology aids learning on condition that it is integrated into the curriculum in a meaningful way (Keengwe & Onchwari, 2009). As has been a long time since technology occupied our lives, it has also become a remedy for classes to attract the interest of students and make lessons more interactive, engaging, and, inescapably, interesting. To do this, teachers should be effective users and designers of technology and integrate it where it is appropriate and necessary. Technology integration can be quite useful to provide feedback to students' work, to enable gamification in the learning process, and to give opportunities to students to create, communicate, and collaborate. Sometimes ironically, technology use in the classroom dominates and overrules teachers' decisions, and it becomes the ultimate aim rather than being a facilitating tool. The formula should be to match each technology-related activity with an acquisition aimed within the framework of a unit. Haphazard use of technology may result in teachers' losing track or students' becoming perplexed. As Schleicher (2018) emphasizes, technology was often limited to supporting existing practices in the past and today's schools need to use the potential of technology to liberate and connect learners in new and powerful ways. In this framework, teachers can make use of technology to design meaningful activities in and out of the classroom.

6. Interpreting data

The emergence of concepts such as big data and learning analytics has increased the possibility of improving learning environments in educational settings. By using available data, educators can guide reform activities in education and propose solutions to problems in teaching and learning conditions (Siemens & Baker, 2012; Siemens & Long, 2011). The profession of teaching requires making a variety of decisions from designing the instruction to assessing student knowledge, from managing the classroom to improving student learning. This being the case, teachers need to found these parameters to a solid basis. An important starting point for giving educational decisions should be the data. The use of the data appropriately requires teachers to have skills and competencies about data literacy in order that they can interpret and rely on that data to execute their plans. Data literacy and the ability to interpret it can help teachers account for their decisions and rationalize their actions. Here, the key to data interpretation should be to have a systematic approach to follow and have a purposeful manner to collect, analyze, and interpret data to arrive at educational decisions. In this way, they can combine the roles of designer, researcher, and a mentor.

Closing Remarks

In conclusion, members of a specific generation are affected by common environmental elements (e.g. dominant cultural, political, historical, social, and technological impacts) that surround them and thus they grow up in line with these reference ranges. Being engulfed in dominant values, certain cultural codes, thought as well as behavior patterns, members of a particular generation naturally develop a kind of common culture and begin to share similar values. The moment they adopt and interiorize shared ideals or morals, in short values, prevalent among peers, the act of socialization begins to make a move. Leading a life under comparable settings and surroundings as well as being exposed to equivalent motives accelerates the constitution of formative life styles that mark a specific generational cohort. In addition, the fact that the members of a generation have similar opportunities provided by the conditions in a particular period of time make way for career opportunities that were previously unimaginable.

Receiving quality education to contribute to the sustainable development is every child's right, and it is mandatory for them to be able to find solutions to the world's problems in a global network of collaboration. Therefore, providing access to quality education within the United Nations' framework of fourth sustainable development goal is crucial. When the issue is addressed in the educational context, we come to the conclusion that we should provide each generation with the opportunities necessary for that particular age to survive, to become successful, and to have good careers. It can also be inferred that the design of educational environments should be inclusive of every individual, regardless of their socioeconomic status, living conditions, and cultural background. Specific to Generation Alpha, 21st-century skills such as critical thinking, communication, collaboration, and creativity have gained further notice. These skills needs to be nurtured in the classes with utmost attention and care to prepare Generation Alpha for the future life and career. To accomplish this, teachers and school administrators should also have these skills and the existing school culture should focus on the constant cultivation of them. Apart from the skills, they need to come across with ample opportunities to internalize flexibility and adaptability, to take initiatives and be self-directed, to be equipped with social and cross-cultural skills, and to sustain their productivity and accountability throughout life by possessing leadership skills and responsibility. These critical points signals the consideration of quality educational design so as not to miss the mark.

References

Bandura, A. (1991). Social cognitive theory of self-regulation. *Organizational Behavior and Human Decision Process*, *50*, 248–287.

Bassham, G., Irwin, W., Nardone, H., & Wallace, J. M. (2013). *Critical thinking: A student's introduction* (5th ed.). USA: McGraw-Hill Companies, Inc.

Battelle for Kids. (2019). Framework for 21st century learning definitions. *Partnership for 21st century learning: A network of Battelle for Kids*. Retrieved from: www.battelleforkids.org.

Beers, S. Z. (2011). *Teaching 21st century skills: An ASCD action tool*. USA: Association for Supervision and Curriculum Development.

Carl, A. E. (2009). *Teacher empowerment through curriculum development: Theory into practice* (3rd ed.). South Africa: Juta and Company Ltd.

Chelimsky, T. D. (1997). The coming transformations in education. In E. Chelimsky & W. Shadish (Eds.), *Evaluation for the twenty-first century* (pp. 1–26). USA: Sage.

Conklin, W. (2012). *Higher-order thinking skills: To develop 21st century learners*. USA: Shell Education.

Delcampo, R. G., Haggerty, L. A., Haney, M. J., & Knippel, L. A. (2011). *Managing the multi-generational workforce: From the GI generation to the millennials*. England: Gower Publishing Limited.

Eaton, S. E. (2018). 21 characteristics of 21st century learners. Retrieved from: http://wp.me/pNAh3-14d.

Fromm, J., & Read, A. (2018). *Marketing to Gen Z: The rules for reaching this vast and very different generation of influencers*. USA: AMACOM.

Gobo, G. (2016). Glocalization: A critical introduction. *European Journal of Cultural and Political Sociology*, *3*(2–3), 381–385.

Gravett, L., & Throckmorton, R. (2007). *Bridging the generation gap: How to get radio babies, boomers, gen Xers, and gen Yers to work together and achieve more*. USA: The Career Press, Inc.

Henger, B., & Henger, J. (2012). *The silent generation*. USA: AuthorHouse.

Jezard, A. (2018). The 3 key skill sets for the workers of 2030 Retrieved from: https://www.weforum.org/agenda/2018/06/the-3-skill-sets-workers-need-to-develop-between-now-and-2030/

Keengwe, J., & Onchwari, G. (2009). Technology and early childhood education: A technology integration professional development model for practicing teachers. *Early Childhood Education Journal*, *37*, 209–218.

Kennedy, I. G., Latham, G., & Jacinto, H. (2016). *Education skills for 21st century teachers: Voices from a global online educators' forum*. Switzerland: Springer International Publishing.

Lancaster, L. C., & Stillman, D. (2002). *When generations collide*. USA: HarperBusiness.

Leaning, M. (2009). Theories and models of media literacy. In Marvus Leaning (Ed.), *Issues in information and media literacy: Criticism, history and policy* (pp. 1–18). USA: Informing Science Press.

Marston, C. (2007). *Motivating the "what's in it for me?" workforce. Manage across the generational divide and increase profits*. USA: John Wiley & Sons, Inc.

McCrindle, M., & Wolfinger, E. (2011). *The ABC of XYZ: Understanding the global generations*. Australia: UNSW Press.

Moore, B. N., & Parker, R. (2015). *Critical thinking* (11th ed.). USA: McGraw-Hill Education.

Parry, E. & Urvin, P. (2010). Generational differences in work values: A review of theory and evidence. *International Journal of Management Reviews*, *13*(1), 79–96.

Patota, N., Schwartz, D. & Schwartz, T. (2007). Leveraging generational differences for productivity gains. *Journal of American Academy of Business, 11*(2), 1–10.

PrincetonOne, & Hobart, B. (2014). Understanding generation Y: What you need to know about the Millennials, 1–11. Retrieved from: http://www.princetonone.com/news/PrincetonOne White Paper2.pdf.

Reis, A. T. (2018). Study on the alpha generation and the reflections of its behavior in the organizational environment. *Quest Journals Journal of Research in Humanities and Social Science, 6*(1), 9–19.

Riedling, A. M. (2007). *An educator's guide to information literacy: What every high school senior needs to know*. USA: Libraries Unlimited.

Robinson, K., & Aronica, L. (2009). *The element: How finding your passion changes everything*. USA: Penguin Books.

Schleicher, A. (2018). *World class: How to build a 21st century school system*. France: OECD Publishing.

Seemiller, C., & Grace, M. (2016). *Generation Z goes to college*. USA: Jossey-Bass.

Seemiller, C., & Grace, M. (2019). *Generation Z: A century in the making*. USA: Routledge.

Siemens, G., & Baker, R. S. (2012). Learning analytics and educational data mining: Towards communication and collaboration. *LAK'12 Proceedings: 2nd International Conference on Learning Analytics and Knowledge*. Vancouver, Canada.

Siemens, G., & Long, P. (2011). Penetrating the fog: Analytics in learning and education. *EDUCAUSE Review, 46*(5), 31–40.

Stiggins, R. J. (1995). Assessment literacy for the 21st century. *Phi Delta Kappan, 77*(3), 238–245.

Tee, W. J. (2018). Project-based learning for building work and life skills in line with TGC and purpose. In Siew Fun Tang & Chee Leong Lim (Eds.), *Preparing the next generation of teachers for 21st century education* (109–125). USA: IGI Global.

Tomlinson, C. A. (2014). *The differentiated classroom: Responding to the needs of all learners*. USA: Association for Supervision and Curriculum Development.

Tomlinson, C. A., & McTighe, J. (2006). *Integrating differentiated instruction and understanding by design*. USA: Association for Supervision and Curriculum Development.

Trilling, B., & Fadel, C. (2009). *21st century skills: Learning for life in our times*. USA: Jossey-Bass.

Turk, V. (2017). Understanding generation alpha. Hotwire The Global Communications Agency Report. Retrieved from: https://cnda.condenast.co.uk/wired/UnderstandingGenerationAlpha.pdf

Underwood, C. (2007). Bridging the generation gaps. *American Gas*, *89*(6), 42–43.

Wiggins, G., & McTighe, J. (2007). *Schooling by design: Mission, action, and achievement*. USA: Association for Supervision and Curriculum Development.

Williams, A. (2015, September 19). Meet alpha: The next 'next' generation. *New York Times*. Retrieved from: https://www.nytimes.com/2015/09/19/fashion/meet-alpha-the-next-next-generation.html.

Williams, K. C., & Page, R. A. (2011). Marketing to the generations. *Journal of Behavioral Studies in Business*, *3*(3), 1–17.

World Economic Forum. (2018). The future of jobs report. Centre for the New Economy and Society. *World Economic Forum*. Retrieved from: https://www.weforum.org/reports/the-future-of-jobs-report-2018.

Zimmerman, B. J. (2000). Attaining self-regulation: A social cognitive perspective. In M. Boekaerts, P. R. Pintrich, & M. Zeidner (Eds.), *Handbook of self-regulation* (13–39). USA: Academic Press.

Ahmet Aydemir

Teaching Generation Alpha

Abstract: Generation Alpha, referred to as Gen Alpha, is the first generation born completely within the 21st century. 2.5 million Alphas are born every week, and by 2025, they will be making up almost 2 billion of earth's population, which by then will exceed 8 billion. As such, it is crucial to understand the dynamics into which this generation is born and the contextual stimuli which will shape this generation. The 21st century, while ripe with innovative digital technologies such as artificial intelligence and augmented and virtual reality, also houses high rates of poverty, overpopulation, pollution, global warming, extinction and war. This chapter explores the social and psychological influences of the current century on Generation Alpha. The chapter also examines the necessary skills teachers must obtain and develop in order to be able to better understand, communicate with and educate Generation Alpha. The chapter thus aims to provide an understanding of the current context of Generation Alpha, and equip the teachers of Generation Alpha with the required competencies to help their students better realize their potentials in the rapidly changing milieu of the 21st century.

Keywords: Generation Alpha, technology, teaching, 21st century

When we look at the history of humankind, we see that each generation is similar to and at the same time different from each other in certain aspects (Bresman & Rao, 2017). Various generations coexist with each other within particular time lines, and thus share some contextual qualities while also differing in their actions and reactions within those contexts.

Generation Alpha, within this framework, shares today's world with Baby Boomers, Generation X (Baby Bust), Millennials (Generation Y) and Generation Z (iGen; Robinson, 2016). As such, in order to understand this upcoming generation, we must first understand what sets it apart from others that share its timeline.

As the offspring's of Millennials, more than 2.5 million Generation Alphas are born every week throughout the world (Sterbenz, 2015). By 2025, when they have all been born, there will be approximately two billion Generation Alphas around the globe (Parsons, 2019; Williams, 2015). Generation Alpha is the first generation that is fully born in the 21st century. It is also the most technologically adept and digitally literate generation to this date. Moreover, it is the generation with the widest access to and most means of reach for information (Williams, 2015).

One of the most crucial factors that sets Generation Alpha apart from others is technology. Generation Alpha is the first generation born fully immersed in technology, social media and digitalization. It is the first generation that regards technology not as a set of tools but as a part of their lives and personalities. They are exposed and so prone to interact with smartphones, tablets and voice assistants from birth. For them, technology is a deeply integrated part of their families and everyday lives (Lavelle, 2019).

One aspect that this integrated technology affects Generation Alpha from birth is their learning methods and education. Up until the 21st century, or even the last decade, people have used real world experiences and stimuli to learn and teach others. With the introduction of digitalization as a disruptive method of education, the way people learn, and so teach others to learn, has started to change. Some Millennials, and a portion of Generation Z, have gone through this change in learning and teaching methods, but Generation Alpha is the first generation that will be educated from childhood to adulthood via next-gen educational technologies. As such, how Generation Alpha experiences the world, and as a result their personality formation, will change with how they learn about life.

So, how will technology enhance the cognitive and intellectual development of Generation Alpha? Technology will provide wider access to information, faster and integrated processing methods, and the means that enable people to work simultaneously as teams. Virtual and augmented reality will allow Generation Alpha to experience real life scenarios in lifelike simulations; 5G networks will provide seamless experiences of connectedness and sharing; and technologies integrated within people's daily lives, such as cellphones, smart watches, smart glasses and other yet to be invented smart devices, will provide immediate and unlimited access to any and every kind of information (Jong-Wha, 2018; Ratcheva & Leopold, 2018). Recent reports show that more than 40 % of children have smartphones and/or tablets (Ofcom, 2016), which implies that Generation Alpha, from birth, will be equipped with a plethora of digital tools to experience learning in an integrated and holistic manner, making them the most technologically adept and so possibly the most formally educated generation ever (Williams, 2015).

One main challenge, then, that the older generations will face when educating, communicating and working with Generation Alpha will be the gap of technological aptitude between them. Generation Alpha will be comprised of people who are born into technology and as such consider it to be an inseparable part of their daily lives (Lavelle, 2019). In essence, people dealing with Generation Alpha on a daily basis will have to get accustomed to and keep up with the rapid digital advances of their era. This will especially hold for teachers, trainers and educators. Not only will they have to be confident in their competence on educational knowledge and skills, they will also have to get to know, and preferably efficiently implement into their lives and teaching methods, the most recent technological developments of the future. They will have to continuously follow global technological and digital trends, be adept at using different social media channels to communicate with and convey messages to Generation Alpha, and be informed on a variety of topics, educational, social and cultural, to be able to teach to a generation that already has access to the majority of world's knowledge on their fingertips from birth (Turk, 2017).

These facts imply that new generation educators will have to be flexible in their communication and teaching methodologies, follow current trends and be adept technology users. A necessary (but probably not sufficient) way to do that will be to accumulate knowledge and develop themselves on 21st-century skills, as by 2022, skill requirements of many jobs will differ significantly (World Economic Forum, 2018). The emphasis on 21st-century skills will have a two-way benefit; first, it will allow teachers to enhance their personal and professional skills based on the requirements of the century, allowing them to do their jobs more efficiently and effectively. Second, since they will be adept at 21st-century skills after learning about them, they will be more competent in teaching these skills to Generation Alpha. This way, they will be able to equip the next generation with the necessary future skills, making them more prepared for professional life and highly employable for next-gen organizations.

21st-Century Teaching Skills

Which 21st-century skills should educators focus on, then, for themselves and their students? One vital set of skills that the teachers should take into account will be critical/analytical thinking, reasoning, evaluation and problem-solving (World Economic Forum, 2018). The new eras will bring with them continuous amounts of change in technology, lifestyles, economies and sociopolitical climates. As such, educators, to be able to navigate in such volatile, uncertain, complex and ambiguous (VUCA environments), will have to be able to evaluate these shifts in a systematic level and manner, and make smart decisions based on their critical thinking and analyses. They will also have to be flexible, proactive and innovative to solve next generation problems, since such rapid changes in unpredictable environments will surely bring about a plethora of new problems. Naturally, they will have to teach Generation Alpha how to do these as well, since they will be the employees who will spend most of their lives continuously adjusting to change.

Another set of skills that educators should focus on is active learning and developing learning strategies (World Economic Forum, 2018). As mentioned, in a context where they have to upkeep with an unceasing plethora of changes, teachers will have to find ways to actively learn each new material and develop strategies to be able to learn from different sources and mediums, educational and otherwise, so that this new data not only stays with them, but builds on pre-existing information in a meaningful way to create cumulative knowledge. They will then have to teach Generation Alpha methods of learning; learning to learn, so to say, in order for them to be able to retain the rain of information they are exposed to from various resources to be able to make sense of it in a useful and consequential manner.

A crucial set of skills at this stage will be technology design and programming (World Economic Forum, 2018). Educators, regardless of the area of expertise, will have to be competent in implementing technology into their educational designs, and programming the necessary software and hardware to support these designs. Technology will be the language of Generation Alpha, and educators will have to speak the same language in order to communicate with them. These skills will also help teachers better design teaching and evaluation methods befitting future eras. It is only natural, then, that they will have to teach Generation Alpha the same skills as to empower them to use programming and technology to the best of their abilities.

Another skill set that the teachers will have to be competent in will be innovation, creativity, originality, ideation and initiative taking (World Economic Forum, 2018). This is because, after being adept at developing learning strategies, technology design and programming, educators will be responsible from making sure that the methods and strategies of learning and teaching they develop are innovative and authentic. Furthermore, being able to take initiative will allow them to put forth bolder and more unconventional ideas fitting Generation Alpha's needs and wishes. These teachers will then need to transfer this knowledge to their students so that the students can become creative innovators who can think outside the box and take initiative to put their ideas into reality.

A final set of skills that educators will need to be experts in will be emotional intelligence, social influence and leadership (World Economic Forum, 2018). Emotional intelligence, defined as "the ability to engage in sophisticated information processing about one's own and others' emotions and the ability to use this information as a guide to thinking and behavior" (Mayer, Salovey & Caruso, 2008, p. 503), and regarded as a set of skills that include emotional awareness, impulse control, motivation, empathy and social relationship management (Goleman, 2012), currently plays and will continue to play a vital role for all occupations including human interaction. By its nature, it is a vital skill that educators should be experts in. It will allow teachers to be able to understand their own feelings and control them. This control will enable them to get less affected from negative emotional states, and to motivate themselves more when they feel positive emotions. Emotional intelligence will also make the teachers be aware of how their students are feeling, which will make them better communicators and educators since they will be better able to understand the needs and wants of their students and thus fine tune their strategies and methods accordingly. With this understanding, they will be able to motivate their students even in environments where there is rapid change, unpredictability and instability. This will, in return, increase their social influence, thereby enhancing their positive effects on students and also peers. As a consequence, they will become better and more competent leaders in their fields. This way, they will be able to better influence their students, communities, schools and other educational shareholders, in other words, the whole education ecosystem, in a manner that is beneficial for all parties involved. The final challenge that educators will face at this stage will be teaching these qualities to their students, since to instill developments in emotional intelligence, social influence and leadership in others, they will have to be confident, creative, authentic and inspiring. Generation Alpha who are students of these teachers will thus be more competent, innovative and influential as individuals.

How should educators, after obtaining 21st-century skills, update their teaching methods to be able to reach Generation Alpha? Generation Alpha's incessant interaction with digital devices will enhance their visual and sensorimotor skills, and hand-eye coordination (Green & Bavelier, 2003; Latham, Patston & Tippett, 2013). Playing games will be a significant part of their learning experience; as traditional methods of learning and teaching become obsolete, gaming will take their place as an effective and addictive education method. The devices they use will get smarter day by day, and thus be able to offer more individualized and personalized services for each user. Augmented and virtual reality will become a part of Generation Alpha's daily lives, and gestural and voice interfaces will take their place among physical and digital interaction, making learning even more interactive and immersive. As such, educators will have to create content that is original, inspiring, interesting and relevant at the same time. They will have to embed various styles and types of technology use into their teaching methods, and be able to effectively reach their students.

To truly reach students, however, it will not be enough for educators to enhance themselves on the aforementioned skills and develop appropriate content and teaching methods. One major issue they will face will be on getting to know the students and their personalities, in other words, student identities. Even now, each of us have several identities, some physical, and some digital, which we choose to share or not with those around us. The overabundance of social media platforms that exists today will likely increase even more with Generation Alpha, as more tailor-made technologies are made available to them. As such, they will have multiple digital identities and footprints. That is why the teachers will not only have to understand who their students are, but also with which identities of the students they are dealing with during their education (Turk, 2017).

The Future of Generation Alpha

As far as their identities go, Generation Alpha will have to be activists, pacifists, freedom fighters, peacekeepers, liberals, conservatives, believers, non-believers, innovators, producers and customers all at the same time. This is because the world we are leaving to Generation Alpha is a tattered mess of chaos. Billions of people try to survive below the poverty threshold; there is an extremely uneven distribution of wealth between nations and societies; and rising trends in extremism continue to bolster culture, religion and gender inequalities. There is an increasing amount of unemployment, especially around youth, and huge disparities for education and employment opportunities between developed and underdeveloped countries. Health issues are threatening all of the world due to the contamination of food and water sources, depletion of natural resources, bio-diversity loss on land and sea, and rise of anti-vaccination movements. Climate change is affecting people and the environment more directly and powerfully each day, especially in the underdeveloped countries. As if these were not enough, there is discrimination, conflict, violence, war, terrorism and fascism (United Nations, 2015). In short, "The survival of many societies, and of the biological support systems of the planet, is at risk." (United Nations, 2015, p. 5).

An individual belonging to Generation Alpha, then, will live in a world in such a dire situation. In that world, in order to survive, that individual will have to embrace many identities. Generation Alpha will have to actively fight for human rights, while pacify those trying to hurt humanity each day. They will have to work diligently in order to stay above the poverty threshold while at the same time trying help those suffering from hunger and thirst. They will have to be liberal and democratic in order to provide equal rights to everyone regardless of gender, religious affiliation, sexual orientation and ethnic background, while also striving to conserve historical and cultural values, traditions and rituals. They will have to find jobs to work in or startup their own jobs, while at the same time try to create job opportunities for their less fortunate unemployed peers.

They will need to use whatever natural or synthetic resources they can to the world survivable and more habitable, yet they will also have to make sure that the generations that come after them have resources to sustain themselves as well. They will be obligated to provide help to those in need while keeping their own health, physical and mental, intact. They will have to strive to stop wars, yet fight for their freedom and rights if and when necessary. In other words, in a world that is heading towards an unsavory destination, they will have to be modern-day super heroes, and save the world.

Understanding Generation Alpha

It is thus an obligation that educators understand each and every identity Generation Alpha embraces well. Teachers should be able to assess and evaluate what Generation Alpha goes through every day, and provide appropriate solutions to their problems as fast as they can. They must also be able to comprehend the uniqueness of the global context that Generation Alpha will be situated in, and guide them accordingly. They must communicate with Generation Alpha in a manner that is interesting, relevant, inclusive, sensitive, inspiring and authentic. They must develop and establish innovative learning methods that will enable Generation Alpha to reach their full potential without compromising their norms and values. And they must do all of this while keeping up with the latest technological, social, cultural and political trends.

An educator's job is never easy, and with Generation Alpha, things will only get trickier. Teachers' journeys with Generation Alpha will be challenging, but this does not necessarily mean that they will not be enjoyable As with every generation, what they expect from their teachers is simple: that they save the world. Thankfully, as Mustafa Kemal Ataturk, the founder of the Republic of Turkey states: "Teachers are the one and only people who save nations." It is thus up to them to save the world by making sure that Generation Alpha is educated to become as powerful and efficient as they can be.

References

Bresman, H., & Rao V. D. (2017). A survey of 19 countries shows how Generations X, Y, and Z are -and aren't- different. *Harvard Business Review*. Retrieved from: https://hbr.org/2017/08/a-survey-of-19-countries shows-how-generations-x-y-and-z-are-and-arent-different.

Goleman, D. (2012). Emotional intelligence: Why it can matter more than IQ. USA: Random House Publishing Group.

Green, C. S., & Bavelier, D. (2003). Action video game modifies visual selective attention. *Nature*, *423*(6939), 534–537. DOI: 10.1038/nature01647

Jong-Wha, L. (2018). This is the key to surviving the age of automation. World Economic Forum. Retrieved from: https://www.weforum.org/agenda/2018/09/education-in-the-age-of-automation

Latham, A. J., Patston, L. L. M., & Tippett, L. J. (2013). The virtual brain: 30 years of video-game play and cognitive abilities. *Frontiers in Psychology*, *4*(629), 1–10. DOI: 10.3389/fpsyg.2013.00629

Lavelle, D. (2019). Move over, millennials and Gen Z – here comes Generation Alpha. *The Guardian*. Retrieved from: https://www.theguardian.com/society/shortcuts/2019/jan/04/move-over-millennials-and-gen-z-here-comes-generation-alpha

Mayer, J. D., Salovey, P., & Caruso, D. R. (2008). Emotional intelligence: New ability or eclectic traits? *American Psychologist*, *63*(6), 503–517.

Ofcom. (2016). Children and parents: Media use and attitudes report. Ofcom. Retrieved from: https://www.ofcom.org.uk/research-and data/media-literacy-research/childrens/children-and-parents-media-use-and-attitudes-report-2018

Parsons, J. (2019). Forget millennials and Gen Z, the rise of 'Generation Alpha' is on the horizon. Metro UK. Retrieved from: https://metro.co.uk/2019/06/20/forget-millennials-gen-z-rise-generation-alpha-horizon-10016963/

Ratcheva, V. S., & Leopold, T. (2018). 5 things to know about the future of jobs. World Economic Forum. Retrieved from: https://www.weforum.org/agenda/2018/09/future-of-jobs-2018-things-to-know/

Robinson, M. T. (2016). The generations: Which generation are you? Retrieved from: https://www.careerplanner.com/Career-Articles/Generations.cfm

Sterbenz, C. (2015). What is Generation Alpha? Business Insider. Retrieved from: https://www.businessinsider.com/generation-alpha-2014-7-2

Turk, V. (2017). Understanding generation alpha. Hotwire The Global Communications Agency Report. Retrieved from: https://cnda.condenast.co.uk/wired/UnderstandingGenerationAlpha.pdf

United Nations. (2015). Transforming our world: The 2030 agenda for sustainable development. Retrieved from: https://www.un.org/en/development/desa/population/migration/generalassembly/docs/globalcompact/A_RES_70_1_E.pdf

Williams, A. (2015). Meet Alpha: The next 'Next Generation'. The New York Times. Retrieved from: https://www.nytimes.com/2015/09/19/fashion/meet-alpha-the-next-next-generation

World Economic Forum. (2018). The future of jobs report. Centre for the New Economy and Society. World Economic Forum. Retrieved from: https://www.weforum.org/reports/the-future-of-jobs-report-2018

Nihal Yurtseven

Enriching Alpha Classes with UbD-Based Instructional Design

Abstract: This chapter is focused on how to design the instruction by using a specific instructional design model, called UbD (Understanding by Design). Children of Generation Alpha, who are born into the digital world, start their education by having a good command of technology and technological devices. With their inborn capacity and sophisticated knowledge for using technology, teaching these children can be both easy and difficult as they can easily be distracted in the learning environment unless they are provided with meaningful tasks, having a patterned connection to each other. As mentioned before, UbD is an instructional design model, consisting of three patterned stages, named as desired results, evidence, and learning plan. Throughout the chapter, teachers of Generation Alpha received information about how to use this model, help their students transfer their knowledge into their daily lives, and create a learning atmosphere for enduring understanding.

Keywords: Generation Alpha, instructional design, UbD, understanding by design

The explosion of knowledge in the 21st century and easy access to every single information rapidly have lit the fuse for the discussions on the effectiveness of existing instructional methodologies and commonly accepted beliefs regarding learning. Daunting as it may seem, children have begun to learn many things that are taught in the classes before they start school. We witness cases in which first-year teachers welcome literate students or, even more notable, students that already know adding or subtracting. Similarly, there are cases in which students are fluent speakers of a foreign language. For this very reason, today's classes should offer more than what students can already find themselves with the help of search engines, YouTube videos, or any kind of learning tools. As the changing world implies, today's classes should have the function to prepare learners to use what they have acquired in the classes in a flexible and independent way. And yet, the critical design of instruction and necessary tools in this process come to the foreground.

What Are the Key Traits of Alpha Children?

As the only generation who has entirely been born to the 21st century, Fourtané (2018) explains the key characteristics of Alpha generation as the following:

- They prefer to acquire knowledge by active learning experiences.
- They would like to know the pragmatic benefit of bodies of knowledge.
- They need learning environments in which their problem-solving and critical-thinking skills are nurtured.
- They never feel afraid of technology, and they always welcome opportunities to use smartphones, tablets, and artificial intelligence.

Understanding: Why Does It Matter?

Be it Alpha or not, every student comes to the class each day with the expectation of learning, and based on the standards, learning occurs, either in a deep or in a superficial way. Defined as surface-level learning by McNair (2019), learners are sometimes only able to recall certain facts or complete assignments without understanding why and applying learning in new situations at production level. However, apart from enabling students simply to succeed in short-term exams, our mission should be to deepen learning in a way in which students experience real learning, internalize facts or opinions, and transfer their knowledge to daily life. These things, as a whole, refer to the term "understanding". Teaching for understanding signals a shift from focusing on pure content coverage without fully engaging students in the learning process to uncovering important and transferable facts in students' minds by their full inclusion (McTighe & Seif, 2014).

Understanding in Six Facets

As educators, although we attach great importance to understanding, we sometimes encounter difficulty in finding a concise definition to it. Understanding is an umbrella term, and it is nearly impossible to fit it into one single definition. However, to concretize understanding is crucial to adjust learning settings accordingly. With six facets of understanding, Wiggins and McTighe (2005) reduce the complexity of the issue and they argue that we can observe the following indicators. If students really understand, they:

- Can **explain** a concept or a principle by making perceptive connections, providing enlightening examples and putting the definitions in their own words.
- Can **interpret** by making meaning of provided data or images, creating analogies and metaphors, and telling a story.
- Can **apply** their knowledge in new and complex contexts independently.
- Can demonstrate **perspective** by seeing the broad picture and looking at the issues critically.

- Can **empathize** with others by putting themselves in someone else's shoes and perceiving sensitively.
- Can have **self-knowledge** by reflecting on their learning and experiences through the process, showing awareness of strengths, weaknesses and habits of mind.

UbD in Brief

As a conceptual framework, teachers should negotiate the needs of their students, the requirements imposed by their institutions, the available resources in their contexts, and their content knowledge to what, when, and especially how to teach (Graff, 2011). Considering the complex nature of teaching, teachers need a comprehensive model, taking all the elements into a frame. Developed by Wiggins and McTighe (1998), UbD offers an instructional design model that takes a three-stage approach to unit planning. UbD is not a level-specific or discipline-specific model to instructional design. Rather, UbD can be used at any level from preschool teaching to graduate education. It fundamentally focuses on seeing the pattern among the desired results of a unit, output to be delivered by the students, and the plan of learning. In the traditional way of teaching, there is a list of subjects to be covered; teachers try to pay utmost attention so as not to miss any piece of information to transmit in the classroom, they provide some hands-on activities so that they keep the students busy, and it ends with an assessment activity that is summative in nature. A serious concern with the traditional approach to teaching is teachers' limited time and authority to craft their programs in accordance with their classes' needs. In this sense, UbD provides teachers with "designer teacher" role that enables them about enriching the learning environment by a thoughtful consideration of student needs, opportunities, and the national framework that every teacher should adhere to.

The Philosophy of Backward Design

With its distinctive manner of planning the instruction, UbD goes off the beaten track and suggests starting planning by reckoning in the evidence of understanding. Wiggins and McTighe (2005) identified backward design as the major contributing factor without which it would seem obscure to figure out whether the students have sufficiently understood. By dint of clarifying the evidence of understanding, teachers can become more focused about their expectations and critical knowledge or skills to be gained throughout the unit. This can help them

Tab. 1: *UbD Template*

Stage 1 Desired Results		
ESTABLISHED GOALS	***Transfer*** *Students will be able to independently use their learning to…*	
	Meaning	
	UNDERSTANDINGS *Students will understand that…*	ESSENTIAL QUESTIONS
	Acquisition	
	Students will know…	*Students will be skilled at…*
Stage 2 - Evidence		
Evaluative Criteria	**Assessment Evidence** PERFORMANCE TASK(S): OTHER EVIDENCE:	
Stage 3 – Learning Plan		
Summary of Key Learning Events and Instruction		

Retrieved from: https://jaymctighe.com/resources/

organize the learning environment in accordance with their expectations of performance as part of collecting evidence.

Backward design also acts as the glue that holds the three stages of planning together by embodying the key expectations and aligning the stages to create a consistent flow of activities and careful selection of content by keeping the desired results and evidence in mind. Contrary to traditional way of planning the instruction, backward design delays the selection of instructional activities, materials and the sequence until elucidating desired results and the necessary assessment tools. The meticulous planning of goals, the judicious selection of the performance task and other assessment tools, and the logical sequencing of the chosen learning activities form the basis of this philosophy that is the fundamental approach to instructional planning. By adopting this kind of an approach, teachers of generation Alpha can design the instruction process step by step without falling outside the scope.

Stage 1: Desired Results

Seen in Tab. 1, the stage of desired results, which includes established goals, transfer, essential questions, understandings, and acquisition, is the starting point in UbD-based instructional design. At this first stage, teachers think about skill-based and knowledge-based acquisitions. After listing them, they try to identify enduring understandings and find essential questions that will guide the students throughout the unit. Big ideas, essential questions, and transfer form the basis of the first stage.

Big Ideas

We can define big ideas as "intellectual linchpins" (McTighe & Wiggins, 1999, 71), which is vital and directly associated with the basic facts or opinions of the unit. Rather than being easily forgotten pieces of information, big ideas are transferable and long-lasting facts standing at the heart of a discipline. Big ideas serve the purpose of students' reaching enduring understandings. In essence, the big ideas of a unit can also be associated with a catchy slogan (e.g. Live on the Edges!; Your home is your world!; Keep calm and travel on!). These slogans can explain a scientific fact or a reality about the topic as well as attracting the attention of students. Here, the focus is to arouse interest in an enjoyable way so that students become involved in the lesson. Depending on the nature of the discipline and considering the age group, teachers can determine a theme, a concept, or sometimes a saying that make the content of the unit more meaningful for the students.

Essential Questions

Regarded as a milestone for UbD, McTighe and Wiggins (2013) formulate essential questions as important, timeless, elemental, foundational, and vital. This formulation opens the window to interrogative and crucial questions to be answered by the students. Although questions that guide (Ex. What is the difference between the words *suddenly* and *immediately*?), hook (Ex. Have you ever seen a celebrity?), lead (Ex. What is the sum of the inner angles of a triangle?) can be good classroom questions, we mean thought-provoking and understanding-focused questions by essential questions. Examples can be various for different disciplines:

- What would happen if bees disappeared from nature? (Preschool, 5 years)
- What are the factors that make skiing easier? (Grade 5, Science, Force and Motion)
- How can we demonstrate the common and different characteristics of two different groups? (Grade 6, Mathematics, Sets)
- How do the characteristics of places affect the formation of the population? (Grade 4, Social Sciences, People, Places and the Environment)
- What do celebrations around the world have in common? (Grade 7, English, Celebrations)

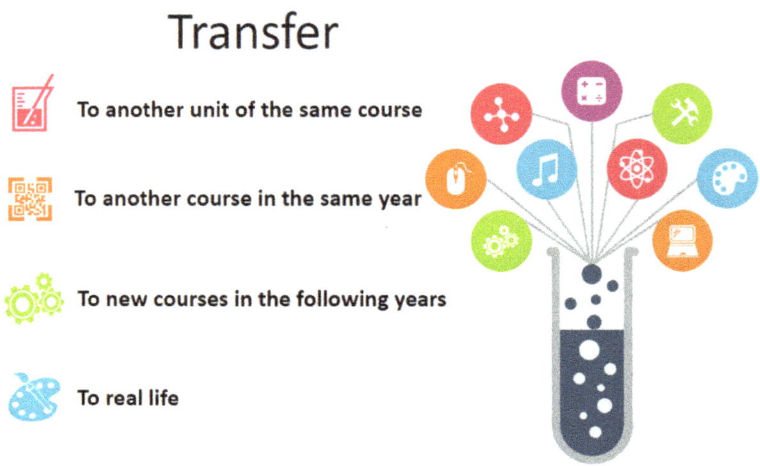

Fig. 1: Transfer

Transfer

Almost all teachers have been asked the following question at least once in their profession: “Teacher, where am I going to use this knowledge?” To put in a nutshell, transfer is a learner’s ability to use the knowledge gained in the classroom in another context, without the support of a teacher or any kind of mentor independently. As can be seen in Fig. 1, transfer can occur in different forms:

Ideally, the transfer literally occurs when the learner manages to use the knowledge gained at school in real life. However, it might not always be possible to find real-life connections in every discipline or every subject/unit of a particular discipline. Finding connections with other units of the same course, with another course that students take in the same year, or the courses to be taken in the following years can be at least more engaging for students. As discussed thoroughly before, it is important for an Alpha learner to know the pragmatic benefit of a unit. Apart from the learner, this will also equip the teacher with a patterned relationship of the content with the outside of the classroom. The following examples can be inspiring for educators to determine transferable knowledge and skills of a unit:

- Students will be able to decide which clothes to wear according to the seasons. (Preschool, 5 years, Clothes)
- Students will know that every person they encounter in the cyber world is not reliable and will communicate with other people by taking this into account. (Grade 5, Social Sciences, Science, Technology and Society)

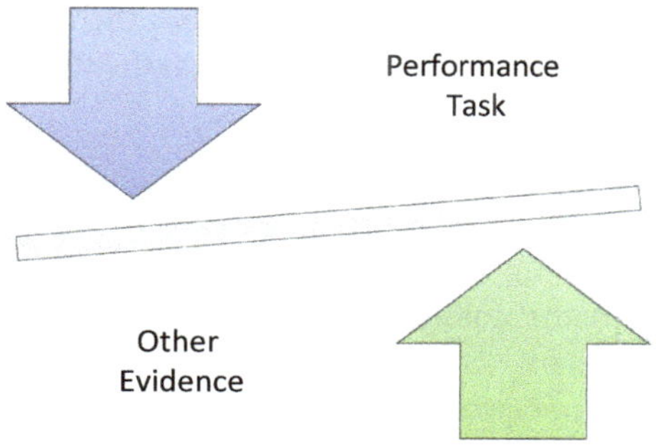

Fig. 2: Evidence

- Students will be able to describe where animals live, what they can do, and how we take care of them. Students will also use their prior knowledge later at Grade 2 "I Love Animals" unit. (Grade 1, English, The Farm)

Stage 2: Evidence

In UbD-based instructional design, the approach to assessment and evaluation is different from the traditional point of view. Metaphorically, the act of testing has a connotation of collecting evidence about student understanding in this approach. Rather than being used as an identifier of student success or failure, assessment tools serve the function of an evidence for the teacher to figure out whether the students have reached meaningful and enduring understandings, as can be examined in Fig. 2:

Performance Task

In spite of the fact that it is not sufficient enough to assess meaningful learning and enduring understanding via performance, it is among the requisites of UbD-based instructional design to ask students to take part in authentic tasks, in which they are able to show their genuine capabilities at least once in every unit. Creating well-established performance tasks that depend upon students' using higher order thinking skills holds paramount importance for teachers to discern whether the expected meaningful learning has occurred or not.

Similar to many other components in the learning process, expectations of teachers from a performance task must be clear to students in its most basic sense. As might be imagined, the unclear announcement of a performance task can be quite confusing for students. To tackle this issue, an abbreviation,

G.R.A.S.P.S is offered to teachers to conceptualize their thoughts. Each letter represents an aspect of the performance and directs the students' attention to the expected performance:

G – Goal: What is the exact purpose of this performance task?
R – Role: What role do you want the student to take?
A – Audience: Who is going to watch the student's performance?
S – Situation: What is the authentic situation that you ask your students to imagine themselves in?
P – Product: What specific product do you want your students to create as part of this performance task?
S – Standards: How are you going to evaluate the performance? What is your success criteria?

In a performance task, determining tangible and transparent expectations paves the way for meaningful learning. This means that students should make sure of what is expected of them to fully demonstrate what they have learned or achieved as well as applying their knowledge in different contexts.

Here is a sample performance task, prepared by using G.R.A.S.P.S chart:

Your goal (G) in this performance task is to investigate the causes and consequences of brain drain. You should choose one of our important scientists who was born in our country and then migrated abroad. You should do a presentation about this person and his/her achievements. In this task, you are a historian (R). As a historian, you will investigate your subject according to the steps of scientific research (S_1). Once you have collected your resources, you should support them with visuals and make them into text and create your slides (P). Your classmates will watch your performance (A). The standards for your performance (S_2):

- Researching and collecting information by making literature search and creating a text (40 points)
- Preparing slides by finding the necessary images (30 points)
- Bibliography (10 points)
- Collaborating with the teacher (10 points)
- Delivering on time (10 points)

Although grounding the assessment on a performance task is a general expectation in UbD-based instructional design, it is important not to miss to assess whether all the acquisitions have been reached. In cases when the performance task does not cover all the acquisitions in the unit, teachers need additional evidence to check whether the students have gained necessary knowledge and skills.

They can use an array of traditional and alternative assessment tools such as quizzes, tests, self-reflection papers, portfolios, structured grids, or even informal observations. After deciding on the evidence, teachers work diligently on the learning plan to offer the students the best learning experiences to become successful in these evidence elements.

Stage 3: Learning Plan

Once the expected outcomes and evidence of understanding is made clear, in Stage 3, teachers spend their time and effort to find the best instructional practices that will engage and empower students in the learning process. Teachers should have students' cognitive activation and experiential learning as their motto at this step. Bearing this in mind, they organize the learning activities and instruction in a way that they foster students' achieving the desired results and succeeding in the performance task. To do this, UbD offers an acronym, WHERETO, to highlight the key considerations in planning learning. In the light of WHERETO principles, teachers can reflect on the following issues:

W – Where and Why: Make sure that students are familiar with the content of the unit, why they are learning it, and how they can use the knowledge they will gain later.

H – Hook: Try to start the unit with a captivating beginning and keep capturing their attention throughout the process. Depending on your talents, interests, and field of expertise, you can use authentic materials such as toys, jokes, drama, and guest speakers in the classroom. Burgess (2012) points out that teachers need to do planning, preparation, and presentation to engage students into their lessons, and the hook of a lesson depends on teacher's choices and creativity.

E – Explore, Experience, Equip: To provide active learning experiences, create opportunities for students to try out, examine, observe, and do experiment where possible. Use a variety of methods, techniques, tools, and materials so that the students can grasp the chance to learn about the know-hows to succeed in the performance task. As Rosenshine (2012) implies, the most effective teachers ensure that students efficiently acquire, rehearse, and connect knowledge with the help of hands-on activities.

R – Reflect, Rethink and Revise: Decide on how often the students should refine the big ideas and reflect on their learning processes. Both their self-reflection and teachers' effective feedback is important to see the general picture in the classroom. Sackstein (2017) emphasizes the value of providing type of structured, clear, reflective, and useful feedback instead of a hurtful, flattering, and ego-stroking ones.

E – Evaluate: At this step, teachers illuminate the ways of evaluation that will accompany the performance task. As a natural feature of UbD, teachers are expected to use various assessment tools, from short quizzes to peer review, encompassing the whole learning process.

T – Tailor the Instruction: To address all the student needs, make a plan of how you can differentiate the instruction throughout the unit. The content of the unit, the learning process, or students' final product can be differentiated regarding students' readiness and achievement levels, learning styles, and interests. Tomlinson (1999; 2014) defines differentiation as a teacher's proactive response to learners' needs. They can make use of a variety of instructional strategies such as learning/interest centers, tiered assignments, small-group instruction, independent study and so forth.

O – Organize the Sequence of Activities: As deepening learning and maximizing student engagement is a promise of UbD, teachers should arrange the learning activities in a way that will fulfil this promise. With the help of this step in the learning plan, teachers decide on how to start the unit, how to order the activities, when to distribute certain materials, when to start the performance task, and how much time to allocate for each piece. This perspective on teaching can also minimize possibility of digressing from the main subject. However, it is important to keep in mind that UbD is not like a strict commitment, and B plans are always welcome in the classroom in case of unexpected or unanticipated situations.

The sample unit plan in Tab. 2 explains how teachers can adapt their plans to UbD-based instructional design:

In brief, understanding the unique preferences, strengths, and weaknesses of every learner is important for the teachers of Generation Alpha. To accomplish this goal, the conceptualization of quality instructional design is the starting point and UbD is a good vehicle to accommodate the learning atmosphere in accordance with student needs and national standards with its three-staged offer via backward design approach. In UbD-based instructional design, the focus is to enable students to reach enduring understandings by which they will be able to make use of what they have learned in the classroom in the new learning environments. By this means, they will actively utilize their skills and knowledge to adapt to a new learning environment.

Tab. 2: *Sample Unit Plan*

Teachers: Esra Kargili Vanaz, Yigit Agan, Seval Unsan		
Grade: 1		
Unit: Shapes		
Stage 1 Desired Results		
Established Goals	***Transfer***	
The aim of this unit is to make students aware of the shapes around them. **Big Idea** World is full of shapes!	Being able to accurately identify shapes is a foundational mathematical skill, and it is quite rewarding for children because their world is full of shapes. Understanding shapes will enable students to be more in tune to the world around them and see the connections between objects as well as being better able to appreciate artistic works.	
	Meaning	
	Understandings	**Essential Questions**
	• Students understand that shapes can be found in the environment all around us.	1. What are some basic shapes? 3. Where can you find shapes?
	Acquisition	
	Students will know:	*Students will be skilled at…*
	• *The names of all the shapes.*	• *Differentiating between different shapes.*
	• *The shapes of objects.*	• *Matching shapes and objects.* • *Talking about the size and type of an object.* • *Using their bodies to create geometric shapes.*
Stage 2 - Evidence		
Evaluative Criteria	**Assessment Evidence**	
Self-correction Peer review	**Performance Task** This performance task will include preparing geometric robot puppets by using colorful cartoons and then talking about their characteristics.	
	GOAL: In this performance task, your goal is to prepare your puppet by using shapes and then make them speak.	
	ROLE: You are a puppeteer. **AUDIENCE:** The audience is your friends.	
	SITUATION: To prepare your puppets individually and present it to your classmates in the classroom. **PRODUCT:** The puppet that you prepared by using shapes that you have learned through the shapes unit.	

(*continued on next page*)

Tab. 2: (continued)

Teachers: Esra Kargili Vanaz, Yigit Agan, Seval Unsan	
	STANDARDS: • Preparing an attractive and colorful puppet. • Naming the shapes which are used while making the puppet. • Finding a creative name for the puppet. **Other Evidence** • Some worksheets which are about shapes. (How Many…?) • Shape Hunt Worksheet.
Stage 3 – Learning Plan	

Where: In this unit students learn to identify the shapes around them. They learn to name the basic shapes like square, circle, triangle, rectangle, oval, diamond, heart and star.

Students have an opportunity to explore/predict manipulate objects to gain an understanding of how shapes embedded in their surrounding environment.

Hook: The use of technology, games, books, hands on manipulation and projected completion of a classroom project.

Engagement: Students do brainstorming activities by answering the essential questions at the beginning of the class.

Revision: Teacher gives individual feedback when the students need. In addition, there will be self-correction and peer review opportunities.

Evaluation: Students will be evaluated through the performance task.

Tailoring: Generally, the teacher uses visual and auditory materials by considering students' learning styles. Therefore, the differentiation of the instruction will be done by differentiating the learning process.

Order/Organization: This unit will be covered in four weeks.

Week 1

- Students will be asked to answer the essential questions. These questions will be discussed in the classroom environment. They will be given clues about the unit.
- Students will be informed about basic shapes like circle, square, rectangle, triangle, oval, diamond, heart, star by the use of materials like cartoons, flashcards, etc.
- Students will revise the numbers.
- Students will be asked to shape their doughs.

Week 2

- In the second week of the unit, shapes will be introduced to students with a presentation. Teacher will give an example for each object from real life materials by showing pictures. And then teacher will want their students to find the shapes in the classroom. They will point and say the name of the shape.
- Student will revise the colors.
- Through the second week, students will be given coloring and drawing papers about shapes.

Tab. 2: (continued)

Teachers: Esra Kargili Vanaz, Yigit Agan, Seval Unsan

- Students will watch videos about shapes.
  - The Shape Song/Super Simple Songs
- Students will do the activities from workbook, page 8–9.
- Students will do the activities from student book, page 12–13.

Week 3

- In the third week of the unit, students will perform their performance tasks. They will prepare their puppets by using their creativity. They will prepare a creative work and give a name to their puppets. They will be asked to give their works to the teacher. Teacher will evaluate their tasks.
- Students will combine the colors and shapes. When they are asked, they will be able to describe the shape like:
- It's a…
  -Blue circle -Pink heart
  -Yellow square -Green star
  -Red triangle -Purple rectangle

Week 4

- Students will watch videos about shapes.
  - The Shape Song 2/Super Simple Songs
- Students will draw the shapes on the whiteboard. Through this activity, students will be able to listen and identify the shape.
- Students will revise the school objects.
- Students will prepare their shape pizzas. They will talk about its recipes.

For Example:

I used ….. squares.

I used …. triangles.

I used …….. circles.

I used…….. rectangles.

Recommendations

- Teachers should proceed with small steps in the process of being a designer-teacher and switching to UbD-based instructional design.
- Working as a team and spending a designated time for collaborative planning will help teachers "understand" other teachers' viewpoints and make sense of the instructional design process.

- It is not an ideal approach to use UbD partially. It is important that teachers should see the patterns among the stages, see the whole picture with the logic of backward design.
- Considering Alpha generation, teachers should place more emphasis on differentiation and tailoring the instruction since they value making their own choices more than any other generation.
- Without ignoring the crucial place of technology in our lives, teachers should try to integrate Web 3.0 tools into lessons so that students can have a personal learning experience.

References

Burges, D. (2012). *Teach like a pirate: Increase student engagement, boost your creativity, and transform your life as an educator*. San Diego, CA: Dave Burgess Consulting, Inc.

Fourtané, S. (2018). Generation Alpha: The children of the millennial. Retrieved from: https://interestingengineering.com/generation-alpha-the-children-of-the-millennial.

Graff, N. (2011). An effective and agonizing way to learn: Backward design and new teachers' preparation for planning curriculum. *Teacher Education Quarterly*, 1, 151–168.

McNair, A. (2019). A meaningful mess: A teacher's guide to student-driven classrooms, authentic learning, student empowerment, and keeping it all together…without losing your mind. USA: Prufrock Press, Inc.

McTighe, J., & Seif, E. (2014). Teaching for understanding: A meaningful education for 21st century learners. Retrieved from: https://www.jaymctighe.com/wp-content/uploads/2011/04/Teaching-for-Understanding.pdf.

McTighe, J., & Wiggins, G. (1999). *Understanding by design: Handbook*. Alexandria, VA: Association for Supervision and Curriculum Development.

McTighe, J., & Wiggins, G. (2013). *Essential questions: Opening doors to student understanding*. Alexandria, VA: Association for Supervision and Curriculum Development.

Rosenshine, B. (2012). Principles of instruction: Research-based strategies that all teachers should know. *American Educator*, 12–19.

Sackstein, S. (2017). *Peer feedback in the classroom: Empowering students to be experts*. Alexandria, VA: Association for Supervision and Curriculum Development.

Tomlinson, C. A.(1999). The differentiated classroom: Responding to the needs of all learners. VA, USA: Association for Supervision and Curriculum Development.

Tomlinson, C. A. (2014). *The differentiated classroom: Responding to the needs of all learners*. Alexandria, VA: Association for Supervision and Curriculum Development.

Wiggins, G., & McTighe, J. (1998). *Understanding by design*. Alexandria, VA: Association for Supervision and Curriculum Development.

Wiggins, G., & McTighe, J. (2005). *Understanding by design: Expanded 2nd edition*. Alexandria, VA: Association for Supervision and Curriculum Development.

Enisa Mede

Fostering Creativity in Alpha Classrooms

Abstract: Creativity is the ability to think in novel and unusual ways about the possible solutions to various problems. Considering creativity instruction, teachers are agents of change who are expected to facilitate independent learning, construct stimulating environments for critical and creative thinking, and role model creativity-fostering behavior. Specifically, how well they play this role relies on whether they demonstrate creativity fostering behavior when interacting with their students. In a creativity-fostering classroom, teachers promote creative thinking by providing choices, rewarding different ideas and products, encouraging sensible risks, and emphasizing students' strengths and interests. In short, teachers are in a strategic position to empower creativity of their students. However, not all teachers are equipped with such capacity-building behavior. They may and may not be conscious of how their own behavior can influence that of their students where creativity is concerned. Therefore, they need be aware of their impact on student creativity, and they also need to be trained to demonstrate creativity fostering behavior in their classroom practices. This chapter aims to emphasize the importance of fostering creativity in classrooms by emphasizing recent theories and approaches for creative pedagogy and provide pedagogical implications on fostering student creativity in alpha classrooms.

Keywords: Generation Alpha, creativity, creative thinking, creative teaching

Creativity is an essential aspect of teaching and learning which influences worldwide educational policy, affects classroom practices and shapes the possibilities of 21st-century learners. The way creativity is defined, nurtured, and linked with real-world problems is rapidly changing the ways contemporary scholars and educators are now approaching creativity in educational contexts.

As creativity has gained increasing importance in education, teachers are expected to foster student creativity demonstrating creativity behavior when interacting with their students. Specifically, fostering creativity is closely related with teacher behaviors including maintaining an open attitude towards creative ideas or behaviors, showing a humanistic student control, being flexible in thinking, and valuing independent thinking (Amabile, Hunnessey, & Grossman, 1986; Erdogdu, 2006; Torrance, 1995). However, it is also a truism that some teachers lack the ability to build such capacity-building behaviors. They may experience some difficulties while trying to shape the behaviors of their students when creativity is concerned. In short, teachers should encourage students to develop their abilities to reason and think creatively. This leads naturally to the question of how teachers can encourage student creativity and which practices and/or activities they should engage their students in to promote creativity in the classroom. This chapter first describes the framework for creative teaching and pedagogy. Then, it summarizes recent approaches and methods to student creativity followed by creativity supporting teacher behaviors. After that, the chapter proposes instructional strategies for fostering student creativity and highlights the importance of creativity for learning. Next, this chapter focuses on creativity and innovation in education. Finally, the chapter suggests a road map and provides pedagogical implications about incorporating creativity in alpha classrooms.

Creative Teaching

Creative teaching can be described in two ways; firstly, teaching creatively and secondly, teaching for creativity. While "teaching creatively" refers to the teacher's use of imaginative approaches to make learning more interesting, engaging, exciting and effective, "teaching for creativity" might best be defined as using forms of teaching that are intended to develop students' own creative thinking and behavior (Morris, 2006). In short, teaching for creativity must involve creative teaching.

Actually, teaching with creativity and teaching for creativity include all the characteristics of good teaching such as high motivation; high expectations; the ability to communicate and listen; and the ability to interest, engage, and inspire. Creative teachers need expertise in their particular fields, and they also need confidence to take risks and to pick up unexpected opportunities for learning. Consequently, all of these require more, not less, expertise of teaching (Morris, 2006).

The Framework of Creative Pedagogy

Considering the aspects of creativity nurtured within education, Lin (2011) proposed a framework of creative pedagogy to display the relationship between creativity and pedagogical practices. Specifically, creative pedagogy describes the practice that enhances creative development based on three interrelated elements: creative teaching, teaching for creativity, and creative learning. Fig. 1 illustrates the interaction between inventive and effective teaching (by the creative facilitator) as well as the creative learning (by the active learner).

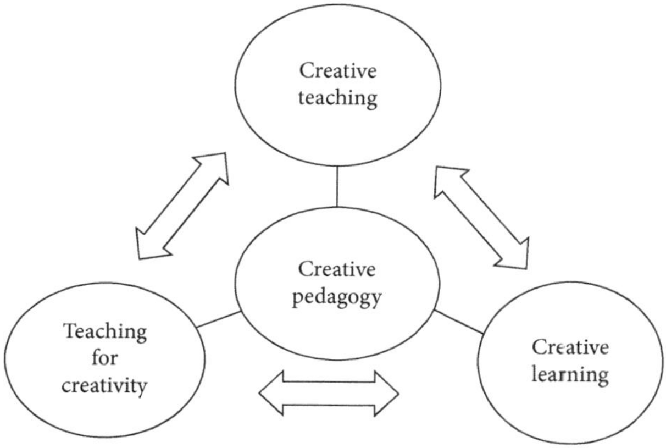

Fig. 1: The Three Elements of Creative Pedagogy

Suggested Approach to Student Creativity

As creativity is so important, how do we facilitate it? Barrett and Donnelly (2008) suggested approaches to foster student creativity. The following eclectic approach in Fig. 2 suggests pathways towards the integration of creative learning strategies into teaching practice:

According to this approach, Pathway 1 includes several techniques that can be used with students quickly in the classroom by teachers. These techniques emphasize group involvement and facilitate meaningful and fun learning by engaging students in role plays, debates, poster presentations, one-to-one tutorials and the use of creative thinking techniques and tools. All these strategies foster student's creative potential as they initiate active, student-centered learning.

Pathway 2 highlights the importance of social and supportive factors such as feedback and support. In other words, formative feedback including self-review and peer review can be incorporated to foster creative performance and talent as well as empower learning relationships. Specifically, through this pathway, students are encouraged to reflect on their creative processes and working relationships, tap into powerful "creative flow" states, develop unique creative thinking and learning styles, and lastly explore strategies for more effective communication and collaboration (Barrett and Donnelly, 2008, p. 6).

Moreover, Pathway 3 deals with the whole change of the curriculum. As Torrance (1997) emphasizes, the focus of education should not be so much on what students learn, but rather on what they can do with their learning. Therefore,

Fig. 2: A Suggested Approach to Facilitating Student Creativity (Barrett & Donnelly, 2008)

creativity embraces the whole curriculum which focuses on teacher education and development, the classroom context, teacher–student relationship, and varying needs of students. It is worth noting that in this pathway, "problem-solving" is equivalent to "resolving anything puzzling or unclear", which is the key function of thinking and active learning.

The Teaching Method of Creative Education

The purpose of creative education is briefly described as "the development of human creativity" (Lee, 2013). Actually, creativity is the essence of personality in the sense that the whole person embraces physical, psychological, emotional, social properties, and fundamental human nature (Lee, 2001). To put it simply, creativity is understood as the universal and holistic aspect of human.

One of the recent and applicable teaching methods has been suggested by Lee (2013), who identifies the method in five stages namely, idea, discovery, digging, manifestation and development. The details of each stage are briefly stated below.

1) *Idea.* The stage of idea is the most fundamental stage as it is accepted as the stage at which creative activity is started. This stage is the start of imagination that is a personal and intuitive action. More specifically, the process of creativity begins by starting the new incorporation of creativity referring to it as the action of imagination.
2) *Discovery.* At this stage, the acceptance of the presented value is done followed by the desire and passion to reach the value. During this stage, the content or object is materialized and creative thinking takes place to find the problem to be solved.
3) *Digging.* As understood from its name, the stage of digging includes the process where the content acquired from the discovery stage is changed to reasonable and systematic conception. Then, the new value can be reached through the goal-oriented and unified conception. In short, during this stage the learner's individual ability can be uniquely built as the external value of the discovery stage is composed and elaborated.
4) *Manifestation.* This stage refers to the process to complete a meaningful content by utilizing dug content as well as making the systematic arrangements. Actually, this stage is the halfway preparation to reach the value of development prior to the last stage of discovery.
5) *Development.* At this stage, there is the completion of creating new value. It is the stage of application to practice and also, the realization of conception by using everyday thinking freely. However, this is not the final accomplishment of the value. Rather, the creative calculation process is an endless continuity of learner's creative ability. Therefore, this five-stage teaching method can be described as unlimited educational possibility of human capability cultivation.

Creativity Supporting Teacher Behaviors

There have been extensive and comprehensive models on creativity-supporting teacher behaviors in literature. One of these is Torrance Incubation Model (Murdock & Keller-Mathers, 2008; Torrance, 1979) which comprises three basic components: (1) heightening anticipation, (2) deepening expectations, and (3) extending the learning. Firstly, the aim of *heightening anticipation* is to give purpose and motivation through warm-ups and activities that generate curiosity and increase the desire to learn the content through confrontation with ambiguities and uncertainties. *Deepening expectations* consists of engagement in the subject through careful analysis of the concepts and ideas based on digging engage learners to take the content beyond what is taught and discussed in the classroom. Finally, *extending the learning* encourages students to take the lead and apply their project in the real-life context to extend the process of learning.

Apart from Incubation Model, nine teacher behaviors on fostering student creativity are listed in a paper, named *Fostering Creativity in the Classroom: General Principles*, by Cropley (1997):

(1) *Independence:* Encouraging students to learn independently.
(2) *Integration:* Having a co-operative, socially integrative style of teaching.
(3) *Motivation:* Emphasizing mastery of factual knowledge, so that students have a solid base for divergent thinking.
(4) *Judgment:* Delaying judging students' ideas until they have been thoroughly worked out and clearly formulated.
(5) *Flexibility:* Encouraging flexible thinking.
(6) *Evaluation:* Promoting self-evaluation in students.
(7) *Question:* Taking students' suggestions and questions seriously.
(8) *Opportunities:* Offering students opportunities to work with a wide variety of materials and under many different conditions.
(9) *Frustration:* Helping students to learn to cope with frustration and failure, so that they have the courage to try the new and unusual.

In addition to these general creativity models, Soh (2000) operationalized these nine principles and developed the Creativity Fostering Teacher Behavior Index (CFTIndex) that highlighted the importance of such behavior as following:

> "Where creativity fostering behavior of teachers is concerned, the lack of suitable measuring instruments will limit the relevant discourse to the philosophical and conceptual levels (which are, of course, important in their own right as a subdomain of creativity research.) But, there is also the need to empirically tests out the theory, an activity that calls for adequate measurement" (Soh, 2000, p. 119).

Based on this perspective, Soh (2000) converted these principles into behavioral statements. Some examples are demonstrated below:

1. Independence: *I encourage students to show me what they have learned on their own.*
2. Integration: *In my class, students have opportunities to share ideas and views.*
3. Motivation: *Learning the basic knowledge/skills well is emphasized in my class.*

4. Judgment: *When my students have some ideas, I get them to explore further before I take a stand.*
5. Flexibility: *In my class, I probe students' idea to encourage thinking.*
6. Evaluation: *I expect my students to check their own work instead of waiting for me to correct them.*
7. Question: *I follow up on my students' suggestions so that they know I take them seriously.*
8. Opportunities: *I encourage my students to try out what they have learned from me in different situations.*
9. Frustration: *My students who are frustrated can come to me for emotional support.*

Instructional Strategies for Fostering Creative Thinking

Of the models that facilitate the development of creative behavior in the classroom, Hong, Hartzell and Green (2009) proposed instructional strategies to empower creative thinking as multiple perspectives in problem-solving, transfer of knowledge to different situations, task commitment, creative skill use, and collaboration which are briefly explained in the following part of this chapter.

1. *Multiple perspectives in problem-solving.* Creative thinkers generate not only novel ideas but multiple, divergent ideas as well (Guilford, 1967). Runco (2003) describes being creative as a type of problem-solving that includes construction of new meaning. Creative thinkers demonstrate abilities in real life problem-solving domains, and they produce original and divergent solutions to problems posed to them (Hong & Milgram, 2008).
2. *Transfer of knowledge and strategies.* Transfer refers to the ability to take knowledge or strategies gained in one situation and apply them to a different situation. With the flexible or divergent use of knowledge, skills, and strategies, students are able to transfer their learning to different situations (Hong, Hartzell & Green, 2009).
3. *Task commitment.* One of the most recent definitions of task commitment has been proposed by Renzulli (2002) who views task commitment as the capacity for high levels of interest, hard work and determination, self-confidence and the drive to achieve, the ability to identify significant problems, and setting high standards for one's work. Feldhusen (1995) emphasizes the importance of students' commitment to contend that students need to develop their creativity and talent. One way of encouraging commitment is providing students with challenging tasks.

4. *Creative skill use.* Engaging students in activities appealing to their interests both in and out of school increases opportunities for them to use creative thinking and skills. Therefore, to help students improve their creative-thinking ability, teachers should provide them with the opportunities to use it.
5. *Collaboration.* Collaboration is one way of developing creative skills and abilities. Brainstorming activities are most commonly used by teachers to foster collaboration and to actively engage students in the creative process.

Creativity and Learning

There is a clear consensus that creativity and learning have a mutually supportive relationship with each other (Dewey, 2007; Guildford, 1950; Ripple, 1977; Beghetto, 2016b). A key question is what is the role of the teachers and students to support creative learning? The following part of this chapter highlights the features of the learning environment that are thought to be supportive of creative learning.

The Role of Teachers

Creativity researchers have outlined the features of supportive teachers' behaviors (Beghetto, 2013; Cropley, 2001; Hong, Hartzell, & Green, 2009; Torrance, 1962) which can be listed as follows:

- establishing improvement-focused learning goals;
- providing opportunities for students to use their imagination while learning;
- encouraging students to take sensible risks and act independently;
- teaching with a more game-like or playful approach;
- providing opportunities for choice and discovery;
- encouraging flexible thinking and confidence in students' ideas;
- treating student questions and ideas (especially unusual and unexpected ones) seriously;
- refraining from premature assessment of students ideas;
- demonstrating a belief that teaching should go beyond imparting simplistic and factual knowledge;
- supporting students when they fail by showing them ways to learn from their mistakes.

Actually, implementing these strategies in the classroom is not that easy particularly in crowded classrooms or classrooms with low-performing students. To foster creativity in the classroom, teachers should have a good understanding of creativity and creative education. Although creative teaching is a challenging process, it should be incorporated in teacher training programs to help teachers develop the knowledge as well as gain the necessary skills and abilities to nurture creativity in the students.

The Role of Students

Apart from teachers, students also play a vital role in establishing a learning environment that fosters creative learning. Students need to be confident, willing to take risks, share ideas as well as listen and support their peers in doing so (Beghetto, 2016). As students are still in the development process of their creativity, this process might seem a bit challenging. Students' creativity may vary, which may take some time for them to regulate how and then they express their creativity (Karwowski, 2017). Therefore, teachers should serve as agents to help students experience, shape, and re-shape their creative behaviors by engaging them in creative activities. According to Morris (2006, p.4) when students are engaged in creative activities, they are likely to…

- *question and challenge.* Creative pupils are curious, question and challenge, and do not necessarily follow the rules.
- *make connections and see relationships.* Creative pupils think laterally and make associations between things that are not usually connected.
- *envision want might be.* They imagine, see possibilities, ask 'what if?', picture alternatives, and look at things from different viewpoints.
- *explore ideas and options.* Creative pupils play with ideas, try alternatives and fresh approaches, keep open minds, and modify their ideas to achieve creative results.
- *reflect critically on ideas, actions and outcomes.* They review progress, invite and use feedback, criticize constructively, and make perceptive observations.

In brief, the behaviors of teachers and students and the interaction amongst them aid with the development of more or less creative environments. Such creative environments can definitely transform the way students acquire education and how they apply it in their real life.

Enabling Innovative Teaching and Creative Learning

Creativity and innovation are interrelated concepts which are not just an opportunity, but a necessity in education. It is obvious that creative learning requires innovative teaching. Innovative teaching includes both the practice of teaching for creativity and of applying innovative techniques to teaching. These aspects serve as basis for educational culture that values creative teaching and learning.

There are various policies and practices that more or less support innovation and creativity in education. Acording to Ferrari, Puchie and Cachia (2009, p.41), looking for manifestations of creativity and education is challenging for several reasons:

- Creativity and innovation are processes which do not always result in tangible outcomes and as a result it can be difficult to find evidence of them.
- Creativity and innovation are exposed to subjectivity, arbitrariness, and interpretation; thus making it challenging to compare data.
- Policies are not necessarily mirrored in practice: encouraging creativity and innovation in policies is not enough, as there is a need for a support mechanism.

Besides policies and practices, other factors such as technology, culture, assessment, individual skills, teaching and learning format, teachers, and tools are also influential in supporting creative learning and innovative teaching (Ferrari, Puchie & Cachia, 2009). These factors are referred as *enablers* which should actively function to enable both students and teachers to be actively involved in the creative and innovative process.

Based on these overviews and the conditions that trigger creativity, innovative teaching and creative learning should be first established and then promoted in the educational environment. Therefore, teachers should be supported by their institutions to be both innovative and creative which will lead the way to bring about new pedagogies and to stimulate change in their classrooms (Ala-Mutka, Punie, & Redecker, 2008).

Integrating Creative Instruction in the Classroom

One of the major questions of creative education is how teachers can integrate creative instruction with the content in their classroom. Drapeau (2004) offers the Creativity Road Map that connects the roads to integrate creative instruction with content. The Creativity Road Map is shown in Fig. 3 below:

Road 1: Targeting Creative Thinking Verbs

The focus of Creativity Road 1 is on creative thinking verbs and verb phrases. Teachers particularly pay attention to the use of verbs in their questions. Specifically, they use creative thinking verbs to access creative thinking. Teachers utilize verbs that encourage multiple answers, various answers, and unusual

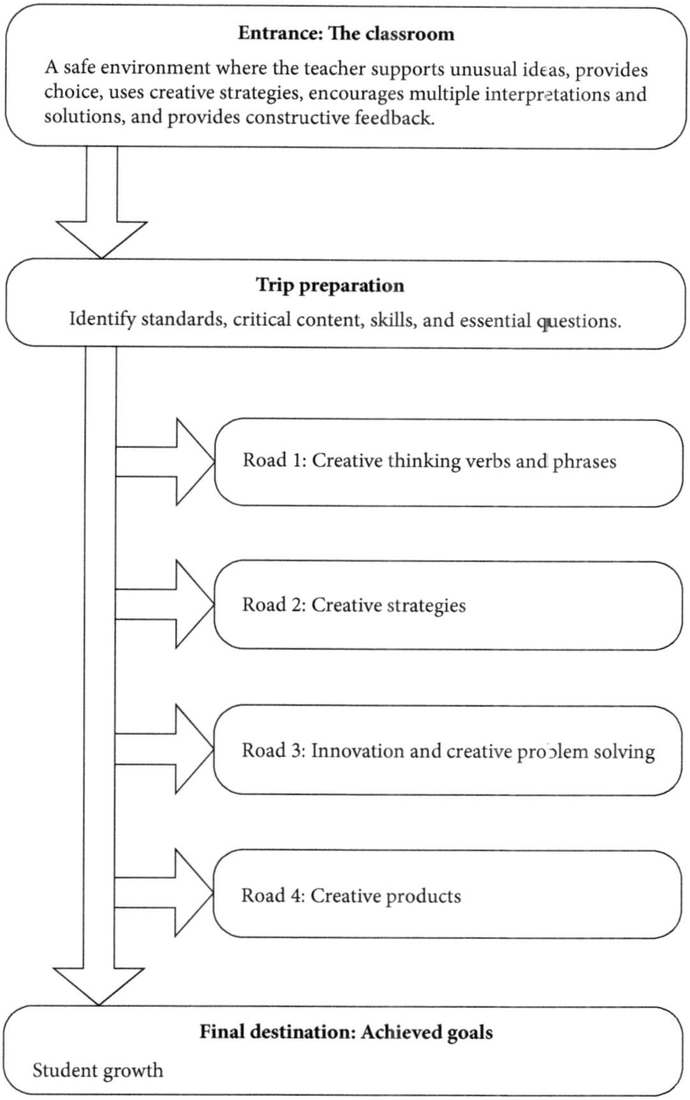

Fig. 3: The Creativity Road Map

answers such as brainstorm, connect, relate, construct, elaborate, embellish, and predict.

Creativity Road 1 is an effective starting point for teachers who are at the beginning stage of using creativity in their classrooms. Actually, this stage requires more than using proper verbs or verb phrases. Encouraging students to interact, share, and exchange ideas would lead to more creative classroom environment.

Road 2: Focusing on Creative Strategies

The purpose of the second road is to design (or redesign) a lesson using instructional tools or strategies and improve the creative skills of students. Specifically, these instructional tools and strategies should be used to promote more than single answer, different kinds of answers, or unusual answers that require group interaction and student engagement. Examples of such creative-promoting activities include webbing, brainstorming, problem-solving, visualizing, considering points of view, transforming, and symbolizing.

Road 3: Using Creative Processes

Creative Road 3 deals with the procedures and processes that students use while they are engaged in creative problem-solving and innovation. This stage is a step-by-step process that encourages creativity. For example, students can identify a specific underlying problem, brainstorm solutions, and try to find out possible solutions.

Road 4: Applying Creative Products

The last road highlights the creative products which can be either simple or sophisticated. These tasks allow varying responses such as written, kinesthetic, visual, and verbal; and they may also include technology. To illustrate, students may be asked to write a digital story or poem elaborating upon characters, settings, content, etc. Actually, creative products can be either small projects or long-term projects conducted in the class, the school, or the whole community.

To summarize, all four roads in the creativity map are interconnected. The teachers decide to use creative-thinking verbs or verb phrases (Road 1), engage students in creative-thinking strategies (Road 2), try to provide creative solutions to identified problems (Road 3) and lastly, culminate in a creative product (Road 4). This road map helps teachers to plan their lessons and determine the type and degree of creativity to be used in their lessons.

Pedagogical Implications to Foster Student Creativity in Alpha Classrooms

We all agree that one of the 21st-century skills is to foster student creativity. Then, the question is what the implications of creative education are. Huai-en (2004) suggests the following implications for creative teaching and learning environments:

1. *Teachers should liberate their minds and give up some control to provide students with more autonomy.* As stated by Huai-en (2004), teachers should liberate their minds and become the directors of their classroom. They should encourage students to think creatively and help them to develop their initiative and enthusiasm. Therefore, teachers should prepare clear lessons plans and design activities that will trigger student creativity.
2. *Teachers should create an open and active classroom atmosphere and allow students to express their mind freely.* It is obvious that positive physical environment has great influence on the achievement of creative activities. Teachers should redesign their classroom in accordance with the activities. For example, students can work in groups while they are engaged in collaborative activities. On the contrary, they can study individually in a writing lesson. In addition, emotional environment is also crucial in a creative classroom. Teachers should create a classroom where students listen to each other and respect their ideas. Students should also feel confident while expressing their ideas, and they should also feel that they are supported by their teachers. As a result, teachers should provide a classroom environment that encourages students' active engagement and creativity.
3. *To foster student creativity, curriculum reform should focus on change and adaptability.* In a creative classroom, the curriculum should be process-based rather than product-based. In other words, students should be involved in processes such as problem-solving, discovery, experimentation and evaluation. 21st-century education highlights the importance of providing students with the opportunity to build programs that meet their particular needs, interests, and abilities. Therefore, principals and schools should be given their liberty and flexibility to develop the curriculum that emphasizes creative education.
4. *Changing the teaching style from text-centered to student-centered is the way to foster student creativity.* Huai-en (2004) stresses that for creative education, teachers should definitely change their teaching style to student-centered. Specifically, teachers should be the facilitators, and they should establish a

comfortable relationship with their students. They should encourage students to think independently and critically and also take risks while learning both from their teacher as well as their peers.

Conclusion

This chapter reflected on the recent theories and pedagogical implications about fostering student creativity in Alpha classrooms. The chapter emphasized framework for creative pedagogy and summarized approaches and methods for a creative classroom. The chapter also focused on creativity supporting teacher behaviors that will lead to creativity for learning. As creativity is closely related with innovation, policies and practices for enabling innovative teaching and creative learning were briefly summarized. Finally, this chapter provided a read map and suggested some pedagogical implications about how to foster student in alpha classrooms. Through the discussions of this chapter, it is intended to clarify the concept of creativity and offer a more comprehensive view of the research implications in fostering student creativity.

References

Ala-Mutka, K., Punie, Y., & Redecker, C. (2008). *ICT for Learning, Innovation and Creativity.* http://ftp.jrc.es/EURdoc/JRC48707.TN.pdf

Amabile, T. M., Hennessey, B. A., & Grossman, B. S. (1986). Social influences on creativity: The effects of contracted-for reward. *Journal of Personality and Social Psychology*, *50*(1), 14–23. DOI: 10.1037/0022-3514.50.1.14

Barrett, T., & Donnelly, R. (2008). Encouraging students' creativity in higher education. In B. Higgs & M. McCarthy (Eds.), *Emerging issues II: The changing roles and identities of teachers and learners in higher education.* Cork: NAIRTL.

Beghetto, R. A. (2013). *Killing ideas softly? The promise and perils of creativity in the classroom*. Charlotte, NC, US: IAP Information Age Publishing.

Beghetto, R. A. (2016). Creative learning: A fresh look. *Journal of Cognitive Education and Psychology*, *15*, 6–23.

Cropley, A. J. (1997). Fostering creativity in the classroom. In M. A. Runco (Ed.), *Creativity research handbook* (pp. 83–114). Cresskill, NJ: Hampton Press.

Cropley, A. J. (2001). *Creativity in education & learning: A guide for teachers and educators*. New York: Routledge.

Dewey, J. (2007). *The school and society*. New York, NY: Cosmo.

Drapeau, P. (2004). *Differentiated instruction: Making it work*. New York, NY: Scholastic.

Erdogdu, M. Y. (2006). Yaratıcılık ile öğretmen davranışları ve akademik başarı arasındaki ilişkiler. *Elektronic Journal of Social Sciences*, *5*(17), 95–106.

Feldhusen, J. F. (1995). Talent development: The new direction in gifted education. *Roeper Review*, *18*(2), 92.

Ferrari, A., Cachia, R., & Punie, Y (2009). *Innovation and Creativity in Education and Training in the EU Member States: Fostering Creative Learning and Supporting Innovative Teaching. Literature Review on Innovation and Creativity in E&T in the EU Member States.* Accessed in 22nd of March 2017, on the Web site of: European Commission, Joint Research Centre, Institute for Prospective Technological Studies: http://ftp.jrc.es/EURdoc/JRC52374_TN.pdf

Guildford, J. P. (1967). Creativity: Yesterday, today and tomorrow. *Journal of Creative Behavior*, *1*(1), 3–14.

Guilford, J. P. (1950). Creativity. *In American Psychologist*, 5,444–454.

Hong, E., Hartzell, S. A., & Greene, M. T. (2009). Fostering creativity in the classroom: Effects of teachers' epistemological beliefs, motivation, and goal orientation. *Journal of Creative Behavior*, *43*, 192–208.

Hong, E., & Milgram, R. M. (2008). *Preventing talent loss*. New York: Routledge.

Huai-en, Y. (2004). To foster students' creativity through classroom teaching. *Proceedings of the Fourth International Conference on ELT in China*. Retrieved September 7, 2019, from http://www.celea.org.cn/pastversion/lw/pdf/YangHuai-en.pdf

Karwowski, M. (2017). Subordinated and rebellious creativity at school. In R. A. Beghetto & B. Sriraman (Eds.), *Creative contradictions in education* (pp. 89–115). Switzerland: Springer.

Lee, J. R. (2001). *Fundamental recognition of creativity*. Seoul: Education & Science Press.

Lee, J. R. (2013). The teaching method of creative education. *Creative Education*, *4*(8), 25–30.

Lin, Y. (2011). Fostering creativity through education-A conceptual framework of creative pedagogy. *Creative Education*, *2*(3), 149–155.

Morris, W. (2006). *Creativity – Its place in education*. Future Edge Ltd based in New Plymouth New Zealand.

Murdock, M., & Keller-Mathers, S. (2008). Teaching and learning creatively with the Torrance Incubation Model: A research and practice update. *International Journal of Creativity and Problem Solving*, *18*(2), 11–33.

Renzulli, J. S. (2002). Emerging conceptions of giftedness: Building a bridge to the new century. *Exceptionality*, *10*, 67–75.

Ripple, R. E. (1977). Communication, education, and creativity. *Contemporary Educational Psychology*, *2*, 219–231.

Runco, M. A. (2003). Education for creative potential. *Scandinavian Journal of Educational Research*, *47*, 317–324. doi: 10.1080/00313830308598

Soh, K. C. (2000). Indexing creativity fostering teacher behavior: A preliminary validation study. *The Journal of Creative Behavior*, *34*(2), 118–134.

Torrance, E. P. (1962). *Guiding creative talent*. New York: Prentice Hall Inc.

Torrance, E. P. (1979). An instructional model for enhancing incubation. *Journal of Creative Behavior*, *13*(1), 23–35.

Torrance, E. P. (1995). Why fly? A philosophy of creativity. Norwood, NJ: Ablex Publishing.

Torrance, E. P. (1997). The nature of creativity as manifest in its testing. In Sternberg, R. J. (Ed.), *The nature of creativity* (pp. 43–75). Cambridge, UK: Cambridge University Press.

Yang, H. E. (2004). To foster students' creativity through classroom teaching. *The Fourth International Conference on ELT*, Beijing.

Ayşin Kaplan-Sayı

Handling Individual Differences in Generation Alpha

Abstract: Generation Alpha is described as the most skillful generation in using technology, also skillful at individualizing the education by using technology according to their needs. So for a teacher eager to handle individual needs by using some differentiation strategies such as Cubing, RAFT, Menu, Choice Boards, this chapter is more important that provides options for each student's learner profile and interest. In this chapter, differentiation and basic concepts, differentiating according to readiness, learning profiles and interest, various differentiation strategies, their example practices and usage of technology for addressing individual differences will be handled. In this way, teachers will have necessary tools for recognizing their students and they will be provided by the 21st-century teaching techniques and practices. Also they can overcome the difficulties of Generation Alpha's changing needs.

Keywords: Generation Alpha, differentiation, individual differences, differentiation strategies

Generation Alpha grows up with smartphones and tablets, and they are able to transfer their thoughts online in just seconds from very young ages on. They spend most of their lives by immersing themselves in technology. As a natural result of today's huge technological advances, they are the most prepared and transformed generation ever. They are mainly described by having an increased screen time, shorter attention span and digital literacy (Nagy and Kölcsey, 2017). "What are the effects of these characteristics in education?" is the key question for educators. The appropriate answer is "Making instruction individualized", for sure. Because, they are exposed to and use individual tools such as YouTube and Instagram that give them endless freedom about choices from birth. So "How can the instruction be individualized?" is the second question. We have many strategies that we can use in educational contexts for making the instruction more individualized such as differentiation that creates space for learners to prefer activities according to their readiness, learning styles and interests especially by using technology or new educational models like Big Picture Model that they are active and they can create their own curriculum. In this chapter, the differentiation strategies, as one of important strategies that we can use with Generation Alpha, and the usage of technology for differentiating the curriculum will be mainly focused; Big Picture Model will be also presented as a way of answering individual needs.

Differentiation and Its Components

Imagine that you go to a restaurant and say that you would like to eat something because you feel hungry and you order a toast.

> The waiter says; "unfortunately we only have hamburger as food."
> After you say you would like to drink orange juice but again,
> The waiter says; "we only sell coke." And you say you would like to go to the restroom for refreshing again the answer is unfortunately,
> "We don't have a restroom because we are a small cafe."

How do you feel in such a case? What do you expect when you enter the café and does the café meet your expectations? All of us expect to get a menu and prefer food and drinks from the menu according to our needs and preferences. If our needs and preferences are not taken into consideration, we think this makes no sense and we should look for different options or places.

Now think about our classrooms and instruction. Do we present menus to our students and can we answer their needs? Do we differentiate our instruction according to their preferences? If we would like to do, let us introduce you the term "differentiation" that can be described as adaptation of the content, process, and product; components of the curriculum according to the readiness, interest, and learning profile of students. Differentiation is an ongoing process in which students' needs are learned and the knowledge acquired by the process used for guiding teaching (Tomlinson, 2007). In the differentiation process, the individual is at the center and all parts of the curriculum are adjusted according to the individual. So, that can also be described as the reflection of democracy into the classroom environment. Generation Alpha has an inquisitive mind, and they want to learn about their interest areas so they need educational settings that appeal to their interests. Because of this need, now a new model "The Big Picture Learning Model" is applied in many schools of USA, Australia and some European countries. According to the model, there are no tests, no grades and for some students no traditional classes to sit through. The program is organized around students' interest, and it is applied as self-paced and self-directed. The main goal is for students to stay motivated and learn by real experiences and doing as well as managing time. Of course, it will get time for educational settings to be prepared as a system like this; so, differentiation can be used as a transitional period strategy for answering students' individual needs. Especially using "digital differentiation" for this group is a must for teachers. Generation Alpha is lucky to have teachers that are digital natives already. They are open-minded and ready to understand the needs of new generation. So, unlike the survey carried out by Pool (2013) % 92 teachers said that they think educational technology tools should be used in classrooms, but only % 14 are integrating technology into their classrooms. By 2025, digital native teachers will integrate the technology into their classes more for the alphas (Culala, 2016).

Differentiation has some components that help us to understand and apply it better. These components can be listed as readiness, interest and learning profile. Readiness covers the student's prior knowledge and the things that s/he can do, the capabilities that s/he has about that topic. Every student has a different background, a different family and a different life style; so, they come to classroom with all these differences. Ideally, a teacher should be aware of these differences and use some tools to assess prior knowledge of students before beginning to study in any unit.

Interest covers the activities the students likes to engage in. It can be varying and endless, but when we think about the whole picture, it can be said that there is nearly no environment that ignores people's interest as much as education and they present options for people. However, in schools we define courses and present students as ready whether they like or not. For softening the situation, the teacher can combine students' interest with the topic that s/he is obliged to cover.

Learning profiles are the ways that a student uses learning. They really have different ways for learning, some of them learn by reading and thinking, some of them learn by analyzing, some of them learn by doing and some of them learn by problem-solving and creating. Or, they learn by using different senses like hearing, seeing or moving. As a teacher this is one of the main tasks to monitor, assess and decide about the learning profiles of students and adjust teaching according to these different profiles.

Generation Alpha is predicted as a knowledgeable one because both their parents and they were born in the technological age. They can reach the information that they wonder in minutes. So measuring their prior knowledge about the topic gains importance for not exposing them to repetition. Especially some technological tools such as Kahoot, Survey Monkey, Google Drive can be used. By using Google Drive, teachers can create a "learn at your own pace" bundle in the folder, so students can have the chance to study content at their own pace and take assessments as they go. Generation Alpha learns by doing; so, as teachers we should provide space to them to experience knowledge and to learn deeply. This leads us to organize problem-based and project-based studies, STEM and inter-disciplined works. While preparing studies for them, integrating activities with technology will appeal to both the different learner profiles and their interest areas. As a matter of the fact, Generation Alpha values smart phones or gadgets more than anything else and spend most of their time by using technology. Interactive white boards, Padlet, Mind Map, Google Sheet and Google Suit will help teachers to catch the different learners.

What about the components related to curriculum and what do mean by content, process and product? Indeed, all these components help us to behave systematically. Teachers can differentiate all the curriculum, but this is not always possible, neither is essential and sustainable. Because, preparing a differentiated plan requires time and preliminary preparation. So, it is important to differentiate essential parts of the curriculum according to the structure of it.

For giving appropriate decisions, it is important to be aware of the definitions. Content is the knowledge on which the topic framed by the curriculum is presented. It covers concepts, principals, theories and also the skills that is expected to be learnt at the end of the unit. The content can also be defined as the input, and it includes tools (textbook, additional reading material, videos, field trips, speakers, demonstrations, conferences or computer programs) that enable students to become familiar with the knowledge.

Process is the facilities provided for students to understand the content. If we only tell students to read a particular text and then ask them to tell us about it, they probably will not grasp the knowledge and tell us. For a real learning process, they handle the knowledge from different aspects in different ways, they have the time to get familiar with it and they are also involved in it. To provide this engagement, teachers can use work-in-pairs activities, work-in-groups strategies, songs, books or movies, prepare debates, design problem–based/project-based learning processes or inquiry-based activities according to learning profiles or interests of students.

Product is a means for a student to demonstrate learning. They present what they understand, and they can do it after learning through writing, drawing, singing, and designing in summary by producing activities. Teachers should know that production is the individual report about a student's learning, because it is very easy to see whether s/he can grasp the knowledge or not. It also helps the student to monitor herself/himself about which parts are understood and which parts are not, and it provides the chance to complete deficiencies. So, it is essential to adapt it according the students' desires, needs and interests.

For differentiating the content for Generation Alpha, teachers can use some websites that can tailor the texts or exercises according to students' levels. Newsela which provides latest articles on current events and presents them at different reading levels or Rewordify which simplifies difficult texts are among the options. This can help students gain access to complex content tasks at

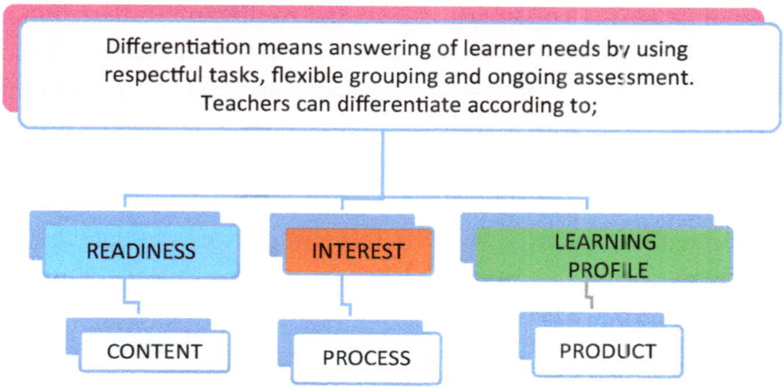

Fig. 1: Differentiation (Tomlinson, 2007).

their comprehension level. NowComment is a website that turns documents into conversations, and ReadTheory is a site that presents an adaptive reading program, based on diagnostic. In addition, Wonderopolis includes texts, each consists of answering a set of questions. Lastly, CommonLit is a site that contains collection of fiction and nonfiction texts according to different levels based on the same theme.

For differentiating the process, teachers can use tools like Poplet for whole class collaboration and Celly for creating a special network of their classes; for assessing the process, Socrative is also a useful app. By using Socrative, the teacher and the students themselves can prepare questions about the topic and identify missing parts of their learning with the instant feedback. ShowMe and ExplainEverything provides the chance to write or draw everything as white boarding apps. The teacher and students can add pictures and sounds in this app and also they can record all these studies. By using these apps, they can create their own lesson videos, as well.

For differentiating product, teachers can use Graphio to ask students to show their understanding, Freemind and Mind Mup. Also, by using Google Classroom, teachers can differentiate the assignments by sending them to only selected students.

We can describe the differentiation better with the graphic in Fig. 1 below:

Differentiation of the Content

Content consists of ideas, concepts, descriptive information and facts. We can adjust the breadth, depth and abstractness of the content according to students' needs. For adjusting the content, it is essential to prepare units around themes or problems. In this way, it becomes easier for students to generalize, integrate and apply the knowledge, and it becomes easier for teachers to differentiate the content. While we differentiate the breadth of the content, we can provide more or less knowledge to students; and for providing more knowledge firstly we can enrich the topic by adding field trips, expert meetings, games and extra studies. We can combine the topic with students' interests, or we can relate the topic with other disciplines. Thus, students can have the chance to learn about the topic more and to apply the knowledge in different contexts.

When we differentiate the depth, we generally use individual studies, projects or research studies. Here, it is aimed that students learn about a topic deeper. So we generally give a research, project, or problem; we enlarge students' knowledge about the topic; and we provide a chance to develop process skills like researching, communicating, collaborating, etc.

In differentiation, supporting the students to learn on their own speed is essential and acceleration is another way of differentiating the subject according to students. With the help of acceleration, the student will be exposed to more knowledge. This will avoid the student to repeat and help her/him to learn about a discipline in a shorter time.

Differentiation of the Process

To differentiate the process, the activities need to be organized mentally in a way that requires more attention. For example, students may need to be challenged with open-ended questions that requires thinking and higher levels of answers. Although instructional strategies vary according to the age of the children and the content of the disciplines, always making children think more abstract and complex is aimed while differentiating the process. In general, we generally add critical thinking and creative thinking to the curriculum to make it more challenging. Additionally, using Bloom's revised taxonomy (2002), Taba's teaching strategy model (1966) and Parnes' creative problem–solving model (1961) can define a way for teachers. By organizing these kinds of activities, we also lead them to research, to explore and to produce. Process is the way that we use while teaching the content. So, problem-based learning, project-based learning, inquiry-based learning, creative-thinking techniques like brainstorming, PMI, Synectic, mind mapping, etc., and collaborative learning are the models or techniques that we can use for differentiating the process.

Differentiation of Product

In general, when we mean product, it is thought as a written study. However, the products should also be adjusted especially for different learning profiles and different interests. Teachers can support their students to produce by reflecting on what they have learned. Students can both master and demonstrate their learning with the help of tasks such as designing games, writing plays, creating videos, etc. Teachers can provide options for products, so each student can choose the task, suitable to her/his learning style. The tasks can include real problems, subjects and people; and they help students to synthesize rather than summarize information and include a self-evaluation process. A final product may be in the form of a demonstration or exhibition. Students can produce a solution to a complex problem, do serious research or write. As Nagy and Kölscey (2017) suggest, these kind of tasks are necessary since Generation Alpha can gather information rapidly and they are good at multitasking. Tasks that require more than one ability and different skills will appeal to them more.

In differentiation, teachers are not obliged to differentiate all components of curriculum – sometimes they differentiate the content, sometimes the process and sometimes only the product. To do this in an easy way, they should know about it well, and they should be skillful at using the technology, because Generation Alpha is the most tech-savvy one and do not know a world without social networking (Schawbel, 2014). Therefore, the term "digital differentiation" comes to scene, as it was mentioned before. Teachers should have the skills for using the platforms like G-Suite or Apple tools for teaching like Geogebra, Puppet Pals, quizlet, etc.; and they should use social networking sites effectively for the sake of teaching and learning.

For differentiating the instruction in a systematic way, it is essential to use some tools that are called differentiation techniques. In this chapter, some extraordinary and user-friendly ones such as cubing, RAFT, menu and choice board models will be presented.

Differentiation Techniques

Cubing Strategy

Cubing is a strategy that compels students to high-level thinking and it requires students to look at a topic from different sides, as can be seen in Fig. 2:

Cubing strategy can be used as an effective tool for handling the topic from six different angles. It provides an image for thinking and can be used as a starting

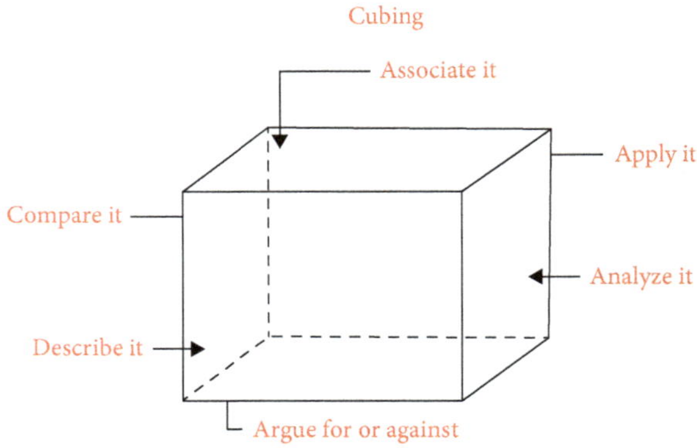

Fig. 2: Cubing

point when teachers want students to analyze or consider various aspects of a topic. Cubes can be used in different forms to clarify the definition of a concept, to reach a conclusion or as a debating tool. Thus, it can be used as a pre-activity tool during the activity or a post-activity tool. When students work with cubes, they use the information in new forms and they are obliged to think divergently. Cubing strategy can be used to differentiate according to interest and readiness. For teaching cubing strategy, it is beneficial to use a common or familiar object like a chocolate. In this way, students will enjoy and grasp the usage of the strategy. The teacher can simply distribute the chocolate to the students and then assign groups to look at (or study) the chocolate from several angles (Prezsler, 2006). Bu using the chocolate as the topic, the teacher can ask students to:

- Describe It: How do you describe a chocolate? Describe its shape, color, smell and taste.
- Compare It: Compare the chocolate with something else. What is it similar to or different from?
- Associate It: What do you associate chocolate with? What does it make you think about?
- Analyze It: Describe the chocolate ingredients. What are its parts? How is it made?
- Apply It: What can you do with a chocolate? How can you use it?
- Argue For or Against It: Present an argument for or against chocolate. After answering the questions, groups can prepare their presentations and share it for 5–8 minutes.

In this activity, the teacher differentiates the process and leads her/his students to higher levels. Teachers can use the cubing strategy for many subjects, and the following stages will help them to apply it effectively:

1. Decide on a topic. For example, Energy. Then plan the time for the activity. How long will it take to complete the activity? Informal cubing activities can easily be accomplished within a class period. However, activities can be extended if research is required.
2. Form the groups based on readiness or interest.

After studying the topic;

- Students will understand that energy is conserved by the transformation of kinetic and potential energy types.
- Students will explain effect of friction force on kinetic energy with examples.

3. Assign each group a perspective from which to explore the topic.

- Describe the energy types; Kinetic energy, potential energy, heat energy, light energy, chemical energy, electrical energy and mechanical energy.
- Compare the kinetic energy to another energy types.
- Associate the energy types with other subjects, issues and events.
- Analyze the energy types by discussing the tools, actions and means of transport.
- Apply the lessons you have learned from studying the energy. How does learning about the energy help you understand subjects, issues and events?
- Argue for or against the friction force. Is the friction force wiped out? Is the friction force more in water or in the air? Take a stand and list your reasons.

4. After a period of time, one of the representatives from each group present their ideas.

Besides the classical cubing strategy mentioned above, teachers of Generation Alpha have different options such as "cube creator". With this tool, teachers can prepare cubes online also in various ways. They can prepare cubes about biographies, and there are different questions that students should answer from easy to difficult. Generally, first side of the cube includes questions like "Who are you writing about?", "When did this person live?", "Where did this person live?" The second side of the cube asks "What were the major events in this person's life?" and in the sixth side a quote from this person is asked. Also it has different types as mystery cube, story cube and create your own cube. In mystery cube, students identify mystery elements, practice using vocabulary from this popular genre, and sort and summarize information. In story cube, students will analyze the story and identify its key elements. In create own your cube type, teachers can prepare the questions. This gives chance to prepare cubes in all topics and asks the questions that teacher or student selects. It is also possible to print the written version of cubes.

RAFT Strategy

RAFT is an acronym that stands for the role of the student, the targeted audience, the format of the production and the topic that is the main idea that we are trying to tell about to the audience. By using RAFT technique, the teacher can organize different works according to the Bloom taxonomy, learning profiles and readiness.

Role. The teacher identifies different roles such as the reporter, scientist, mother, eyewitness, an object or an animal for the students.

Audience. The teacher defines the audience that the students prepare her/his work to present them. It can be the teacher, other students, a parent, people in the community, an editor, another object, another animal, etc.

Format. It is the way in which the students will convey the message or the main idea. The teacher presents manty options such as a poster, a letter, an article, a report, a poem, a monologue, a picture, a song, etc.

Topic. It is the message to the audience and the main idea. The topic can be about a situation, about a subject or about a person. Here, the teacher presents many options such as protect our environment, provide food and shelters for street animals, technology that surrounded our life, a famous mathematician, Second World War, etc.

There is an example of a simple RAFT on Snow White and Seven Dwarfs. It aims to help students to handle the events from different angles. After completing the RAFT as reading objectives:

- Students will read for pleasure and to acquire information.
- Students will show comprehension by retelling and acting out events in the story.
- Students will recognize story problems or plot.
- As writing objectives.
- Students will inform, explain, describe or narrate.
- Students will write to entertain.
- Students will write by thinking flexible.
- Students will use vivid language.

Tab. 1: *The RAFT Sample*

Role	Audience	Format	Topic
Dwarfs	Snow white	1–2 minute conversation	Don't open the door and don't talk to strangers to save your life.
The stepmother of Snow white	Defense attorney	1–2 minute conversation	Help me! I am innocent.
Father of snow white	Public	Warning posters	Marry with the right people if you want to be happy.
Mirror	Journalist	Memoir Letter	The queen's passionate from beginning to end.

For Generation Alpha, webquest or bookwidget can be used which provide a flexible schedule for students to use RAFT technique as in Tab. 1. A webquest is a tool that a teacher can design a lesson in six dimensions such as welcome, introduction, task, process, evaluation and conclusion. Webquest is developed by Dodge (1995) in which the students can learn mostly from internet sources by searching in an interactive way. It generally begins with a problem; tasks are described in process part; generally a standardized rubric is prepared in evaluation part; and it is finished by a conclusion activity in which all the learnings are summarized and generalized. Webquest is like a blog where we can add different website URLs or videos designed specifically for a topic. Teachers can use Zunal WebQuest Maker and WebQuest.Org to create their webquests.

Bookwidget is a tool that helps teachers to prepare their interactive ibooks. BookWidget is a platform that lets educators create interactive activities and engaging teaching material to be used on iPads, Android tablets, Chromebooks, Macs or PCs (www.techlearning.com). By using bookwidgets they can create puzzles, flashcards and games on different subjects. There are 40 different types of activities available in bookwidgets. They can prepare tests, quizzes and follow their students' answer and progression. By using bookwidgets, teachers can differentiate according to readiness, learning profiles and learning time. Event students especially Generation Alpha can prepare their ibooks by using bookwidgets because they like being independent and make their own decisions. So according to the identified outcomes, they can choose their own content and they can prepare their own activities. In my opinion, this will provide a chance for them to support their entrepreneurship.

Menu Strategy

Menu is another strategy that teachers can use to present options to students. A menu presents many options for students to provide the outcomes of the course. Class periods for menus are so flexible that teachers can design menus for only one lesson, for a week or even for a month. The first step for preparing menus is to decide the essential requirements, knowledge and skills; and then teachers should follow the steps presented below:

1. Clarifying the essential elements of a lesson or unit.
2. Preparing an imperative assignment that reflects the minimum requirements of the lesson. These tasks are marked by 2 points in 2-5-8 menus.
3. Creating negotiables which are based on main or imperative assignments or projects. These negotiables often require students to go beyond the basic levels of Bloom's taxonomy. For example, they often include activities that require synthesis, analysis or evaluation. These are the tasks generally marked by 5 points.
4. Presenting a final optional section that offers students the opportunity for enrichment. The optional section often reflects activities that students can use for extra credit. These are the tasks generally marked by 8 points.

There are many kinds of menus such as 2-5-8 menus, tic-tac-toe menus and list menus. In 2-5-8 menus, tasks are organized from easy to difficult and marked according to their easiness or hardness. The student should reach 10 points. One of the 5-pointed task is obligatory. In tic-tac-toe menus, the teacher shows the starting point and decides the activities that should be done first and then students should form a tic-tac-toe across or down. In list menu, all the tasks presented as a list and all tasks are marked according to their easiness or hardness. The students should reach 100 points in a period of time.

As an example, for 2-5-8 menu on folk tales:

Folk tales usually follow a predictable pattern. The stories often start very quickly so children are drawn into the story with ease. The characters are simplistic, and they progress through the tale the plots often seem predictable. Most problems do not get resolved in a happy ending. Reading objectives covered through this menu and activities:

- Students will read from a variety of genre for pleasure and to acquire information.
- Students will interpret figurative language and multiple meaning words.

Tab. 2: *The 2-5-8 Sample*

Direction: Choose two activities from the menu below. The activities must total 10 points.

2 Points

Complete a story map for your folk tale.
Make a poster that shows the elements found in folk tales.

5 Points

Design a survey to discover your classmates' favorite folk tale. Record your data and design a way to present it.
Design a diorama that shows setting and characters in your folk tale.
Make a Venn diagram that compares folk tales to tall tales.
Create a book cover for a folk tale of your choice.

8 Points

Turn one of your favorite folk tales into a play. Submit your script to your teacher.
Create your own folk tale. Include a story map and rough draft your ideas.
(Westpal, 2007).

- Students will show comprehension by retelling and acting out events in the story.
- Students will recognize story problems or plot.
- Students will represent textual information by using story maps.
- Students will compare literary work with another.
- Students will recognize distinguishing features of folk tales.
- Students will compare different forms of story (Written versus performed).

Writing objectives covered through this menu and activities:

- Students will inform, explain, describe or narrate.
- Students will write to entertain.
- Students will revise drafts.
- Students will use vivid language.

Students can complete the menu in 1–2 weeks. Students are given the menu as the unit is started, and the teacher discusses the product options on the menu. As the different options are discussed, students will choose products that add a total of 10 points. As the lessons progress through the week, the teacher and students refer back to the options associated with the content being taught. For 1–2 days, the teacher chooses the activity from the menu with the entire class as described in Tab. 2:

Choice Boards

Choice boards provide the opportunity to master a variety of tasks that allow students to master the skills throughout the course. With these tasks, students can also enhance their understanding of concepts. Students either choose from the board or are assigned to three adjacent or diagonal tasks to complete. Choice boards address student' readiness, interest or learning preferences. They are easily adapted to a subject area.

While preparing choice boards, the steps that teachers should follow can be listed as below:

1. Identify the outcomes of the unit.
2. Use assessment data to determine student's readiness, learning profiles and interests.
3. Design nine different tasks.
4. Select one obligatory task for all students. Place it in the center of the board.
5. Arrange tasks on a choice board.
6. Select one required task for all students. Place it in the center of the board.
7. Ask students to complete three tasks, one of which must be the task in the middle square. The three tasks should complete a Tic-Tac-Toe row.

Teachers can also adapt the strategy according to the group or their working style. They can assign tasks according to the readiness, so the teacher can prepare other choice boards. As can be seen in the sample choice board in Tab. 3, they can create choice boards according to learning profiles such as kinesthetic, auditory or visual, or they can even prepare tasks based on multiple intelligences, allowing students to complete any three tasks.

The outcomes of the topic are:

- Compare the basic forms of the substances.
- Give examples of different forms of the same substance.
- Make simple experiments about the reactions and actions of substances.
- Explain the substances' transformation with the reasons.

Teachers can also digitalize the menus, choice boards by using G-suite tools for Generation Alpha. By using G-Suite, menus and choice boards can become interactive, digital and more dynamic. With digital tools, it is possible to make menus and choice boards more creative and interactive. By using Google Docs, teachers can prepare menus and choice boards; and they can add links, rubrics, images, video and more into their menus. Teachers can also integrate Chrome apps into their digital menus like Canva, Flipgrid, Powtoon, Google

Tab. 3: *Sample Choice Board*

Define solid, liquid and gas. Draw a picture to illustrate each word.	Draw a chart of transformations of substances into different forms.	Do simple experiments that is given in your course book that shows the transformations of substances
Classify the task cards on objects according to their forms as solid, liquid and gas. Write your own examples for each form.	Free Choice	Illustrate conditions of substances melt, freeze, evaporate, condense and sublimate in everyday life. You need two examples for each.
Decide the actions of substances according to their forms: melting, freezing, evaporation, condensation, sublimation.	Play the game Recall or Recall Challenge. (The game is like Taboo, but you need to match up substance forms and their actions according to different situations.)	Complete the puzzle and then create a puzzle of your own.

Slides, Wevideo, Storybird, Buncee or Animoto. With these apps, they can prepare collaborative works. Using these kind of tools helps teachers differentiate according to readiness; learning profile also interest because these tools appeal to all kinds of learning profiles and having the chance to choose the task make the learning differentiated according to the levels. While students are preparing their products, they are free about the subject that helps them receive different materials according to their interests.

Assessment in a Differentiated Classroom

In a differentiated classroom, assessment is constant, which helps teacher to design the further steps of teaching. It presents information about student's pre-knowledge, ongoing process and the gains as well as the students' personality characteristics. Assessment aims to demonstrate the missing parts and increasing success in differentiation. It does not promote peer competition or labelling students with grades. Rather, students are assessed to contribute to their growth.

In differentiation, readiness is assessed to define the student's situation about any topic. In readiness, students' knowledge about concepts, content and skills are measured and this data is used for identifying the learning goals. In interest, assessment interest surveys, interest centers and self-selection projects topics can be used. Learning profiles can be assessed and students' areas of strength and weaknesses, work preferences and learning profiles inventories can help us to organize the studies according to the learning profiles.

Assessment and instruction are interwoven in differentiation, so readiness is assessed both at the beginning of an instructional unit or in sequence. Any method, strategy or process to determine a student's current level of readiness or interest in order to plan for appropriate instruction can be used as pre-assessment. Pre-tests, know-want to know-learned (KWL) charts, checklists, observation-evaluation and questioning can be used as tools.

Pre-assessment;

- Reports the learning gaps,
- Presents information about students' situation and for choosing the appropriate activities,
- Helps teachers to see the differences of each student and present data for planning,
- Helps teachers to design and prepare activities that are meaningful and challenging,
- Presents a way for using the instructional time effectively.

As pre-assessment tools, especially for assessing readiness, teachers can use digital tools like Answergarden. It is a tool for using brainstorming and to see the pre-knowledge of students. Teacher asks a question and students post their answers on it. The answers can be printed as a poster or in Wordle format. Todaysmeet can also be used for pre-assessment. It is a kind of tool called as chatroom, by which students discuss topics, brainstorm or answer the questions.

Formative Assessment

Formative assessment is used for getting information about students' progress and identify whether the instruction period is effective or not. Peer evaluation, self-evaluation, observation, quizzes, questioning, portfolio check, journal entries and three-minute pause strategy can be used as formative assessment tools. Peer evaluations and self-evaluations are especially important for Generation Alpha which includes independent learners. The three-minute pause technique is an alternative in which the teacher asks one to three questions at any point during the lesson. Students answer one or more of the questions in writing on a ½ sheet of paper. Then the teacher reviews the answers and revises the upcoming lessons according to these answers. Volunteers can also read their statements at that time and teaching can be adjusted "on the fly". The statements can be such as;

- I was surprised about
- I became more aware of…
- I want to know more about…

Formative assessment is a kind of assessment process that

- presents regular feedback and provides evidence of progress;
- helps teachers to organize instruction meaningfully and provide information; about students' misconceptions;
- helps students to build on previous knowledge and skills;
- makes teaching parallel with the curricular outcomes.

Seesaw is one of the best tools that can be used for Generation Alpha as a formative assessment tool. Students can organize their portfolio there, and their friends can comment on their studies. Also teachers and parents can examine all students' works from Seesaw which is a kind of electronic portfolio tool. Nearpod is a summative assessment tool where teachers can prepare interactive PowerPoints that include notes, videos, questions, exams, etc. Teachers can examine student's answers and analyze whether the subject is understood or not.

Summative Assessment

Summative Assessment is the assessment that shows the last situation of students after the learning period is completed. It should match the material which is taught and should align with the outcomes. It is a means to determine a student's mastery and understanding of information, skills, concepts or processes. Unit tests, performance tasks, products or exhibits, demonstrations and portfolios review can be used as tools. A summative assessment:

- helps teachers to see the result and decide students' exit achievement;
- helps students to see their progress and final situation.

Socrative is an online exam tool that gives instant feedback to students as part of summative assessment. Generally it is the most difficult part for teachers to give feedback to their students. By using Socrative, they can see their rights and mistakes by answering the questions that the teacher prepare. Pool everywhere is another tool where we can prepare surveys or ask questions online. Triventy, Quizizz and Quizlet are the other tools that teachers can use digitally for assessing the performance of Generation Alpha. While assessing Generation Alpha, it is also important to use pre-assessment, formative assessment and summative assessment and making it seems more effective by using the abovementioned digital tools.

References

Class Tech Tips: Use Book Widgets to Create Interactive Activities for iPad, Chromebooks and More! Retrieved June 5, https://www.techlearning.com/tl-advisor-blog/11471

Culala, H. C. D. (2016). Educating generation alpha: What are the demands of the 21st century workforce? Plenary speech delivered at Digital Education Show Asia Kuala Lumpur Convention Centre (KLCC), Kuala Lumpur, Malaysia.

Dodge, B. (1995). Web quests: A technique for Internet-based learning. *Distance Educator*, *1*(2), 10–13.

Krathwohl, D. R. (2002). A revision of Bloom's taxonomy: An overview. *Theory into Practice*, *41*(4), 212–218.

Nagy, A., & Kölcsey, A. (2017). Generation Alpha: Marketing or science. *Acta Techologica Dubnicae*, *7*(1), 107–115. DOI: 10.1515/atd-2017-0007.

Parnes, S. J. (1961). Effects of extended effort in creative problem solving. *Journal of Educational Psychology*, *52*(3), 117–122. DOI: 10.1037/h0044650.

Prezsler, J. (2006). Strategies That Differentiate Instruction. Retrieved July 29, https://www.tie.net/wp-content/uploads/2018/09/9StrategiesThatDiffInst4_12BookletReduced.pdf

Schwabel, D. (2014). Predictions for Generation Alpha. Retrieved July 25, danschawbel.com/blog/5-predictions-for-generation-alpha

Student Choice and Differentiation with Menus. Retrieved July 20, 2019 https://www.therouttymathteacher.com/2017/10/student-choice-and-differentiation-with-menus.html

Taba, H. (1966). Teaching Strategies and Cognitive Functioning in Elementary School Children. Retrieved June 20, 2019. https://files.eric.ed.gov/fulltext/ED025448.pdf

Tomlinson, C. A. (2007). Öğrenci Gereksinimlerine Göre Farklılaştırılmış Eğitim. Çev. Diye Kültürlerarası İletişim Hizmetleri. 2. Baskı, Sev Yayıncılık.

Westphal, L. (2007). *Differentiating Instruction with Menus: Language Arts (Grades 3–5)*. USA: Prufrock Press Inc.

Sabiha Dulay

Managing Alpha Classrooms

Abstract: Classroom management does not only mean to sit quietly or do whatever teachers require from students, but it consists of creating a classroom environment that supports both academic and emotional learning. For Generation Alpha, teachers might feel helpless in finding ways to teach students to take responsibility of their own learning. Compared to X, Y, and Z generation, this generation have some specific and distinct needs, and as a result, the way it has always been done may not work anymore. This chapter aimed to help teachers learn how to adapt their classroom management strategies regarding needs and interests of them. Self-management is one of the effective ways for teachers to become a mentor or a guide. Self-management strategies can foster students' independence, self-monitoring and self-evaluation. They help students to complete tasks and be active in the class. In this way, teachers adapt the ways to facilitate learning while children are exploring or creating in the classroom. This chapter also tried to help teachers gain an understanding about creating a classroom environment, which fosters creativity, leadership skills and critical thinking of Generation Alpha. The chapter also tried to help teachers learn the ways to turn their traditional classroom management strategies to self-management strategies, which enhance collaboration and innovation via changing norms and let students create and explore.

Keywords: Generation Alpha, classroom management, self-management, self-management strategies

Compared to X, Y and Z generation, Alpha generation have some distinct needs, and as a result, the way it has always been done may not work anymore. The traditional classroom management methods need to change in education to gain this generation. In this context, teachers will need to consider innovative and creative ways to teach the content and to integrate technology in their teaching-learning environment which will foster creativity, critical thinking and problem-solving. Teachers need to learn the ways to become a mentor or facilitator while the new generation explores or creates in the classroom. This chapter aims to help teachers learn how to adapt their classroom management strategies in accordance with needs and interests of Generation Alpha. Self-management is one of the effective ways for teachers to become a mentor or a guide. Self-management strategies can foster students' independence, self-monitoring and self-evaluation. They help students to complete tasks independently and be active in taking responsibility for their own behaviors. Consequently, teachers need to facilitate learning through self-management strategies which enhance collaboration and innovation.

The Challenge of Future Classroom Management: How Will Teachers Be Ready?

You have probably designed your whole lesson carefully, and you have planned how much time you spend on every activity, task or game. You think you are ready for everything you will encounter in the class. But, whatever happened and you realize that you are spending your most of the time on dealing with students' behavioral problems. Some of them are walking or sleeping, the others are speaking, even crying! In order to be an effective classroom manager, teachers need to see the whole picture in classroom management. Classroom management is a broad term including many different aspects of teaching-learning process such as setting rules and procedures, building positive relations, constructing a classroom environment which encourage cognitive, social and physical development of students.

In many researches, classroom management is the top problem indicated by teachers (Çetin, 2009; Flores & Day, 2006; Ritter & Hancock, 2007). Because of management problems, teacher may feel overwhelmed, as well as losing their joy and creativity (Greenberg, Putman, & Walsh, 2014; McCauley-Cate, 2003). The reality shock teachers encounter in their first days causes them to spend their time on dealing with discipline problems rather than flourishing teaching and learning. This power struggle might end with a mindset that tough control is the only way to manage. However, trying to take students under control did not work in the past and is not going to work in the future. Classroom management is not about managing students, but teachers' behaviors towards creating an environment that fosters academic, social-emotional learning and self-management skills of students (Bluestein, 2014; Evertson & Weinstein, 2006).

Classroom management is not only a crucial part of an effective learning environment, but also a challenge for teachers (Flores & Day, 2006; Goddard, O'Brien, & Goddard, 2006; Jones, 2006; Ritter & Hancock, 2007). One of the reasons for this challenge is that classroom management is covered as an elective or single credit lesson in a way that instruction is generally disconnected from practice in preservice teacher education (Evertson & Emmer, 2013; Garrahy, Cothran, & Kulinna, 2005). Therefore, teachers have to learn many things by trial and error (Flores & Day, 2006; Garrahy et al., 2005), and might feel ineffective in finding solutions to problems that they face in classrooms (Pellegrino, 2010).

Managing classrooms effectively is getting harder for teachers nowadays since today's students are not interested in traditional way of teaching and learning. They are known as Generation Alpha or Generation Glass. These children were born in 2010 and are now in classrooms. Compared to X, Y and Z generation, this generation has different needs, interests and skills. As a result, it might not be possible for teachers to manage Alpha classrooms by thinking the previous generations' needs or using teaching materials. Teachers need to find innovative and creative ways to teach the content, and to integrate technology in their teaching-learning environment. But it does not mean that teachers have to forget what they know about teaching profession and classroom management. Teachers should be there in order to facilitate students to get right knowledge since they are not the only one to deliver the knowledge. By constructing a classroom management strategy that encourages flexibility, collaboration, creativity and problem-solving, teachers can be effective in Alpha classrooms.

Managing should not be something teachers decide or handle on their own; instead, students should be included into managing process (Miller, 2016). Teachers help students to learn how to manage their own behavior and work independently. Self-management is the most basic 21st-century skill and includes self-confidence, self-reliance, responsibility and independence (Coil, 2012). When we consider Generation Alpha, creativity, leadership and autonomy for decision-making are among the basic behavioral characteristics of them (Reis, 2018). As a result, developing self-management skills of students will be the most required component of classrooms. As the more independent and cooperative students are, the less time teachers will put out fires the more they will teach (Bluestein, 2014 pp. 42). In self-managed classes teachers need to focus on developing 4Cs and 1R – collaboration, communication, creativity, critical thinking, and reflection- (McNair, 2019). So, what does a self-managed classroom look like?

What Does a Self-Managed Classroom Look Like?

One of the fundamental goals of education is to help students to become more independent and take the responsibility for their own actions. Self-management is an effective way of becoming self-directed and enables students to gain independence and responsibility. Hence, a self-managed classroom creates a safe, collaborative and active classroom environment that builds students' self-control. However, it should not be considered that this class will manage on its own and students do not need teachers. Rather, in self-managed classes students should learn how to take responsibility for their actions. In this process, teachers need to guide and facilitate learning for students.

Taking responsibility and developing independence as two self-management skills go hand in hand (Coil, 2012). In Alpha classrooms, students need to be self-managed individuals in order to keep up with the changing world. As students develop the personal qualities to manage their learning, they can apply the same skills to situations outside the classroom (Dembo & Seli, 2012). In order to create a self-managed environment in their classes, teachers need to involve students into management process. It can be succeeded through giving students power within limitations such as letting them construct their own rules or giving controlled choices for tasks, assignments or materials. Thus, teachers need to adapt their classroom management strategies to self-managed classes. Here are six tips for self-managing classes in Fig. 1:

1. Being Visible and Accessible

Teachers can convey many messages to students via physical presence. Teachers' physical presence includes body language, voice and proximity. As mentioned previously, students need more support from teachers in order to gain confidence in working independently on a task in self-managed classrooms. Therefore, a visible and accessible teacher is an important component for guiding students and facilitating learning in this kind of a classroom. Visible and accessible teachers are always there to monitor progress and offer support if students need help. How can a teacher be visible and accessible? Using proximity by walking around, making eye contact, giving reminders and explanations to assist students' work independently are the simple acts to make teachers visible and accessible in the class.

Being visible and accessible are mostly required for Alpha classrooms since these students are not spoon-fed; instead, they need to create and apply what they learn. Teachers need to find opportunities to let students work independently and make their own choices. After giving simple and clear directions, teachers may say *"If you need my support, I will be there, but if you don't need my support, you can keep on working."* Accordingly, students can learn how to work independently in groups or individually. But, teachers should keep on guiding without distracting students. Teachers can construct a safe and respectful classroom environment by using body language and voice while students are working collaboratively. Making eye contact, using gestures and mimics, as well as using a calm tone of voice will be the effective ways for building self-managed and welcoming classes without speaking.

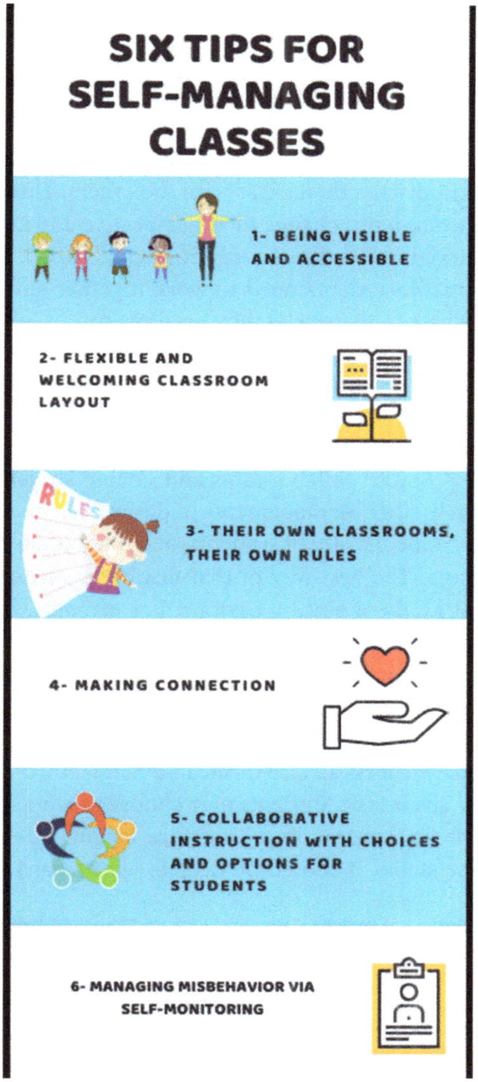

Fig. 1: Six Tips for Self-Managing Classes

2. Flexible and Welcoming Classroom Layout

Layout of the classroom includes the elements such as heat, light, sound, cleanliness, color, materials, order of seating and class size. In order to manage Alpha classrooms effectively, these components should be designed in a way that encourage collaboration, accessibility and flexibility. Collaboration encourages students to share and discuss their ideas with the others. These interactions can provide new ideas to students, change their perspective and also create the sense of identity and belonging for the classroom (Ralph, 2019). In a collaborative classroom environment, students need to work together and access the things (e.g. frequently used areas, materials) they need easily.

Teachers should organize Alpha classrooms which should enable students' collaboration during group or individual tasks. Teachers as a guide and students as an active participant of teaching and learning process should easily be able to move and follow what is going on in the classroom. Changing seating arrangements can promote collaboration and enable students to discuss different ideas with each other. Arrangements of desks (e.g., circles, U-shapes) can be done in regards to the density of students, activities and interaction between teachers and students. The best way of that flexible classroom environment is to include different kinds of seating options. For example, balls and cushions can be used as seats. Students can choose which seat they want, as a result they will feel relaxed and enjoy being in the classroom. Giving students the power to choose what type of seating helps them learn best will encourage independency in making their own decisions, and taking responsibility for their own choices. In addition, teachers can also create independent work stations in which students work on a given task. Students may choose to work by sitting at a desk or chair, lying on the floor or standing. Therefore, layout of a self-managed classroom should not be stable, it should be flexible with regard to students' needs and interests.

Alpha classrooms should be welcoming and lively to engage students into learning. Teachers may hang students work or visual materials on the walls, but they should be careful so as not to distract students' attention. Terada (2018) suggests teachers to keep 20 to 50 percent of wall space clear and fill the rest with student work. Seeing their works on the walls will make students feel belonged in the classroom. The sense of belongingness may promote students' ownership of maintaining the quality of classroom environment. Teachers should share the responsibility between students; thus, every student has different duty or responsibility in the class. Students can work together to maintain classroom environment physically and emotionally safe, positive, neat and organized

(Berger, Strasser, & Woodfin, 2015). Working together and taking responsibility for their actions will promote students' self-confidence and self-discipline. In order to create that classroom environment, teachers need to discuss the expectations and roles of every student, and let students share their ideas. Reflection is the crucial part in self-managed classes. Hence, teachers should spare time on students' reflection. This kind of classroom may seem to be chaotic and frightening for teachers, but they can coach students by giving clear directions and setting effective rules. The following reflection questions can help students think about their learning experience.

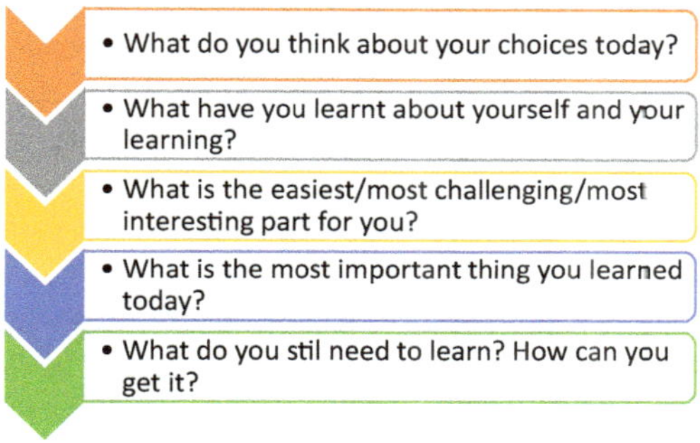

3. *Their Own Classes, Their Own Rules*

Rules are generally defined as desired expectations for behaviors in the classroom. They provide a structured learning environment in which students can feel safe and focused (Levin and Nolan, 2010; Vijayan, Chakravarthi, & Philips, bgrbfrvxa,). Classroom rules are effective tools to convey appropriate behaviors for students of all ages. However, rules should not be a long list of prohibition starting with "Don't". Rather, rules should be simple, positive and state the appropriate behavior (Bluestein, 2014). Long lists given by teachers will not help students to self-manage their own behavior. In this context, rules should be discussed democratically, and students involve this process actively (Cangelosi, 2016; Finger & Bamford, 2010; Marzano, Marzano, & Pickering, 2008). Establishing rules democratically allows teachers and students to discuss the underlying reasons for behaviors they are responsible in the class.

In self-managed Alpha classrooms, setting rules democratically is important, but letting students build their own rules is more important. In order to involve students into the process of setting rules and routines, teachers can start with a *brainstorming session.* Accordingly, teachers require students to work in pairs and come up with ideas for the following questions.

- *What are the situations that you learn best?*
- *What kind of behavior do you need in classrooms?*
- *What makes you distracted from learning?*
- *What happens when a friend breaks the rules?*
- *What are the main challenges for creating safe and respectful classroom atmosphere?*

Students consider, discuss and write their ideas on sheets. After discussion, the next step should be reflection. Teachers ask each group's or student's ideas and discuss them with the class. In reflection, teachers should be effective facilitators. As a facilitator, teachers ask each group's ideas on rules, then he/she starts a whole class discussion. Students discuss the positive and negative consequences or challenges for their ideas, or even they can vote the rules. Finally, they construct their own rules. There should be a consensus on rules and consequences. At the end of this process, students will take the power to manage themselves with their own rules. When students are involved to create rules, they are more likely to follow them. Here are the strategies that can be used to construct rules in self-managing classes:

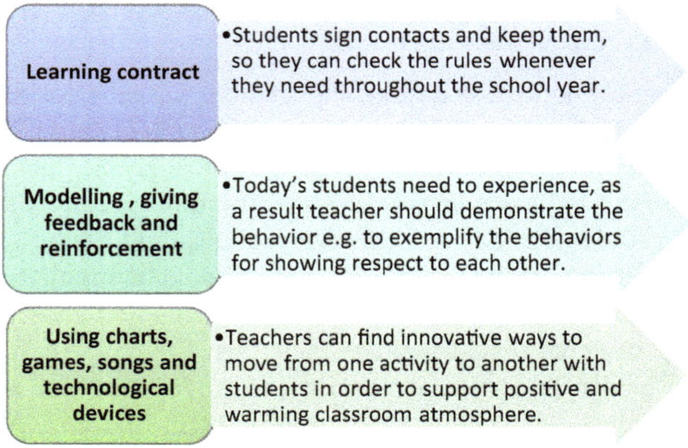

For Alpha classrooms, students need to learn how to use frequently used areas and materials particularly technological devices, and how to manage classroom discussions and work on a task without disturbing the others. Apart from rules, routines including transitions, opening and closing of lessons also make classroom manageable. Berger et al. (2015) suggest to lesson with a striking activity or to close lesson with a reflection including writing the most important thing they learn today, repeating the homework and making a prediction what will be the next steps. These strategies will provide effective time management. However, in order to make students join into active management, they will need to trust teachers. Thus, making connection is the other important component for building self-managed classes.

4. *Making Connections*

Some teachers believe that being "firm" may be necessary to gain the authority over students. However, making meaningful connection with students are necessary for effective classroom management (Hardgrove, 2008; Harris, 2005). Connecting can lead to a decrease in a wide range of risk factors including students' disruptive and violent behavior (Blum, McNeely, & Rinehart, 2004). Once students know that you care or value them, many problems will be solved easily. Students begin to obey rules willingly instead of resistance since they feel teachers recognize them as an individual.

To build a self-managed classroom where students are engaged, and self-motivated while working actively and collaboratively, fostering good relationships with students is the foundation of success (Berger et. al, 2015). Teachers' behaviors that build trust and a sense of belonging will foster engagement in self-managed classrooms. When teachers know students well (e.g. their interests, needs, problems, learning style…), they can provide personally meaningful incentives to motive and give support with regard to their needs. Teachers can build positive relationships with students through caring and valuing, learning their names, talking about their needs, interests and lives outside of school, being fair, and avoiding prejudice. Positive and trustworthy classroom atmosphere will make a major contribution to effective instruction. Here are some recommendations to make emotional connections with students:

- Record their birthdays and organize simple celebration parties for the ones who were born in the same month.
- Get information about their hobbies and interests, and use that knowledge while designing activities or giving rewards.
- Talk about their daily routines and life at home in break times.
- Celebrate their achievements (e.g. sportive or academic achievements) in the classroom.

5. *Flexible and Collaborative Instruction with Choices and Options for Students*

A self-managed classroom fosters flexible, collaborative and active learning through giving students choices and options. Thus, teachers should differentiate learning in accordance with needs and learning styles of students. In order to differentiate learning and provide meaningful experiences, teachers should find creative and innovative ways through which students can combine theory and practice. For various learning experiences, teachers can provide flexible learning goals and assignments based on students' needs, interests and abilities. Using digital and visual materials, gaming, coding and activities based on problem-solving need to be preferred in these classes. YouTube or other video platforms, research tasks on various topics, blogs or tablets can be used to keep students engaged and interested in class. Teachers can give the basic principles or learning goals for the assignments, and let students decide their own ways such as using videos, visual materials, role playing, research projects or anything else. Students' sense of having control and of making choices in the classroom are mostly linked with engagement and learning (Hoy & Weinstein, 2006).

Self-managed classrooms help students learn about their own social and academic strengths and contribute to the class in varied ways depending on their speed and independence (Berger et al., 2015). The best way to ensure that each student gets what he/she needs is to use different techniques, rather than one strategy that fits everyone (Ralph, 2019). This also enhances collaboration. For example, teachers can let students work on a project by writing, drawing, acting or coding. Working groups is an effective way for collaboration. Students can discuss and exchange information within their own groups or between the other groups.

Apart from differentiating activities in regards to students' needs and interests, teachers need to catch students' attention and keep them alert during the classes. In order to catch and maintain attention, teachers use various reinforcers. However, teacher should be careful about using reinforcers since they may cast a cloud on learning goals. Thus, there are some steps teachers can follow in giving reinforcers. Firstly, reinforcers such as rewards or praises should not be vague, and students need to see the connection between their choices and what they earn as a result (Bluestein, 2014). Secondly, they should be reachable for each student. If they believe they will not get any reward no matter how much they try, they will stop trying. Thirdly, reinforcement should be interesting and meaningful rather than just telling you're good, and give opportunity to students to take responsibility for their actions. National Center on Intensive Intervention (2015) suggests different reinforcers teacher can use in regards to needs and interests, as can be seen in Tab. 1.

Tab. 1: *Types of Reinforcers*

Tangible	Activity-based	Social	Intangible
Token, stickers, posters, prize from a prize box, coloring page, books.	Extra time on computer, silent reading time, allowed to be leader, given a classroom job, assisting secretary or teacher.	Tell a joke, lunch with teacher, game with a friend.	Verbal praise, smiles, giving eye contact, positive comment on work.

6. *Managing Misbehavior via Self-Monitoring*

Misbehaviors are not something that should be avoided in classrooms. Rather, they are inseparable parts of classroom management strategies. The main focus should not be on the occurrence of misbehaviors, but on how to manage them effectively. Teachers should be calm and not take students' behaviors personally. They should try to understand the main cause of these behaviors before focusing on the interventions. Listening to students and asking them what happened are necessary steps to discover the underlying reasons. Using descriptive language rather than judgmental one, using presence (e.g. proximity, body language, voice or eye contact), and keeping away from power struggles are some tools for external control teacher can use to manage behavioral problems.

However, in self-managed classrooms internal control is required more. Thus, self-monitoring may be an effective way of self-management to build self-control. Self-monitoring consists of two parts as measurement and evaluation: students *(i)* measure and record their behaviors, and *(ii)* compare that behavior to a predetermined standard (Loftin, Gibb, & Skiba, 2005). Teachers need to prepare a self-monitoring plan in which students are able to recognize the occurrence of target/desired behaviors. These plans may take many forms. Koegel, Koegel and Parks (1995) have outlined five general steps to teach self-management. These are: (1) operationally define the target behavior; (2) identify functional reinforcers; (3) design or choose a self-management method or device; (4) teach the individual to use the self-management device; and (5) teach self-management independence. Grueasko-Moore, Dupaul and White (2006) suggest a self-management plan including three phases as monitoring, fading and transition while Lane, Menzies, Bruhn and Cronobori (2011) outline six steps to implement a self-monitoring plan as follows:

- *Establish prerequisite conditions:* The students should learn and perform the target behavior in self-monitoring form.

- *Identify and define behaviors:* The target behavior should be clearly defined by providing students with examples.
- *Design procedures and monitoring form:* Create a self-monitoring form which should include specific time windows, and lists to record the target behavior.
- *Teach procedures to students:* Use appropriate instructional strategy (discussion, modelling, coaching, role playing, etc.) to teach the students how to use self-monitoring form.
- *Monitor progress:* The teacher can also fill in the same self-monitoring form to monitor and reward students.
- *Conduct maintenance and follow-up:* As the ultimate goal is for students to demonstrate the desired behavior across all settings, praise and rewards should be used regularly.

Self-managed classrooms generally foster personally constructed interventions based on students' needs and teachers' expectations. Therefore, teachers can constitute their own self-monitoring plan in regards to the needs of their own classrooms. No matter which plan they follow, they should start with defining target behavior(s) clearly, and practice that behavior. There should be a consensus between teachers' expectations and students' understanding about target behavior(s). After defining target behavior(s), second step is designing or choosing a self-monitoring tool. In this step, it may be helpful to use different tools such as checklists, rubrics or scales. But they should be so simple and clear that students can understand how to use. Teachers also inform students that they will be recording their behaviors to compare the results.

Students are required to observe their behavior and fill in the self-management form by considering what they did, what they did not, and what they can do more. Self-monitoring should begin with teacher support until they are accustomed to fill in the form independently. If students' recording match that of teacher, teacher allow students to choose a reward or a reinforcer. Giving information about the form and leaving students to monitor their own behaviors will be ineffective without the reflection part. Teachers should engage students into a discussion in order to make them see how well they reach their learning goal. Only then can they apply the same behaviors to situations outside the class. Accordingly, self-monitoring form should be used for teaching various skills to students. For example, maintaining attention, completing an assignment, remaining on task or tracking progress toward a goal (Bell, Magill, Carter, & Lane, 2013). The following self-monitoring form in Tab. 2 can be an example for teachers to create their self-monitoring forms:

Tab. 2: *Self-Management Form*

Self-Management Form			
Name:		**Date:**	
My goal is: I will ….			
Behavior	**Time/Date**	**Time/Date**	**Time/Date**
	How well did I…		
	Excellent Fair Needs Improvement	Excellent Fair Needs Improvement	Excellent Fair Needs Improvement
I met my goal (yes or no):			

Tab. 3: *Self-Evaluation Form*

Describe the situation that happened.		
What caused you to get angry?		
I made a choice: Was it positive or negative? **Circle the choice that you made**	**Positive choices:** - My choice was to take deep breathe. - My choice was to count to one hundred. **Negative choices:** - My choice was to use inappropriate language - My choice was to harm another student.	**Describe why your choice was positive or negative**
I stayed in control	**YES**	**NO**

After self-monitoring, students should evaluate their performance with teachers. Here is an example of a self-evaluation form used by a child with anger problem in Tab. 3 (OSEP, 2016 pp. 6):

Consequently, students will be an active participant in their own learning through gaining responsibility for measuring their own behaviors. In order to help students to find their way in a complicated and changing world, teachers need to help students gain self-management skills. Thus, it will begin in the classrooms. Generation Alpha need opportunities to be active in taking responsibility for their own actions, that is, self-management. In order to turn their classes into self-managing classes, teachers should follow the steps that are discussed in this chapter. They need to be visible and accessible, to create flexible and welcoming classroom layout, to let them create their own rules, to make connection, to provide collaborative instruction and options for students, and to manage misbehavior via self-monitoring. When students gain self-managed skills which can foster independence, self-evaluation and innovative practices in classrooms, they will more likely use these behaviors to the situations outside the class. Thus, they can manage the difficulties they encounter more creatively and confidently in this complicated and changing world.

References

Bell, L., Magill, L., Carter, E. W., & Lane, K. L. (2013). Self-monitoring equipping students to manage their own behavior in the classroom. Tennessee Vanderbilt University: Department of Education.

Berger, R., Strasser, D., & Woodfin, L. (2015). *Management in active classroom*. USA: EL Education Inc. – EL Ed Publications.

Bluestein, J. (2014). *Managing 21st century classrooms: How do I avoid ineffective classroom management practices?* USA: ASCD.

Blum, R. W., McNeely, C., & Rinehart, P. M. (2004). *Improving the odds: The untapped power of schools to improve the health of teens*. Minneapolis, MN: Center for Adolescent Health and Development, University of Minnesota.

Cangelosi, J. S. (2016). *Sınıf yönetimi stratejileri: Öğrencilerin işbirliği yapmalarını sağlama ve bu işbirliğini devam ettirme* (Çev. Ed. R. Hoş & M. Toprak). Nobel.

Çetin, F. (2009). *Eğitim fakültelerinde görev yapan öğretim elemanlarının sınıf yönetimi ile ilgili davranışlarının incelenmesi* (Yayımlanmamış doktora tezi). Gazi Üniversitesi, Ankara.

Coil, C. (2012). Building connections: Developing 21st century self-management skills for gifted students. *Texas Association of the Gifted and Talented*, *33*(3), 9–14.

Dembo, M. H., & Seli, H. (2012). *Motivation and learning strategies for college success: A focus on self-regulated learning*. USA: Routledge.

Evertson, C., & Emmer, E. (2013). *Classroom management for elementary teachers* (9th ed.). USA: Pearson.

Evertson, C. M., & Weinstein, C. S. (Eds.). (2006). *Handbook of classroom management: Research, practice, and contemporary issues*. Routledge.

Finger, J., & Bamford, B. (2010). *Sınıf yönetimi stratejileri öğretmen kılavuzu* (Çev. Ed. T. Karaköse). Nobel.

Flores, M. A., & Day, C. (2006). Contexts which shape and reshape new teachers' identities: A multi-perspective study. *Teaching and Teacher Education*, *22*(2), 219–232.

Garrahy, D. A., Cothran, D. J., & Kulinna, P. H. (2005). Voices from the trenches: An exploration of teachers' management knowledge. *The Journal of Educational Research*, *99*(1), 56–63.

Goddard, R., O'brien, P., & Goddard, M. (2006). Work environment predictors of beginning teacher burnout. *British Educational Research Journal*, *32*(6), 857–874.

Greenberg, J., Putman, H., & Walsh, K. (2014). Training our future teachers: Classroom management. Revised. *National Council on Teacher Quality*, 1, 1–54.

Grueasko-Moore, S., DuPaul, G., & White, G. (2006). The effects of self-management in general education classrooms on the organizational skills of adolescents with ADHD. *Behavior Modification*, *30*(2), 159–183. DOI: 10.1177/0145445503259387.

Hardgrove, P. C. (2008). *An investigation of the life experiences and beliefs of teachers exhibiting effective classroom management behaviors in diverse urban schools* (Unpublished doctoral dissertation), Lamar University.

Harris, S. (2005). *BRAVO teacher! Building relationships with actions that value others*. Larchmont, NY: Eye on Education.

Hoy, A. W., & Weinstein, C. S. (2006). Student and teacher perspectives on classroom management. In C. Evertson & C. Weinstein (Eds.), *Handbook of classroom management: Research, practice, and contemporary issues* (pp. 181–222). Mahwah, NJ: Lawrence Erlbaum Associates.

Jones, V. (2006). How do teachers learn to be effective classroom managers? In C. Evertson & C. Weinstein (Eds.), *Handbook of classroom management: Research, practice, and contemporary issues* (pp. 887–908). Mahwah, NJ: Lawrence Erlbaum Associates.

Koegel, R. L., Koegel, L. K., & Parks, D. R. (1995). "Teach the individual" model of generalization: Autonomy through self-management. In R. L. Koegel & L. K. Koegel (Eds.), *Teaching children with autism: Strategies for initiating positive interactions and improving learning opportunities* (pp. 67–77). Baltimore, MD: Paul H. Brookes Publishing Company.

Lane, K. L., Menzies, H., Bruhn, A., & Crnobori, M. (2011). *Managing challenging behaviors in schools: Research-based strategies that work*. New York, NY: Guilford Press.

Levin, J., & Nolan, J. F. (2010). *Principles of Classroom Management* (Sixth ed.). Boston: Pearson Education Inc.

Loftin, R. L., Gibb, A. C., & Skiba, R. (2005). Using self-monitoring strategies to address behavior and academic issues. *Impact*, *18*(2), 12–13.

Marzano, R. J., Marzano, J. S., & Pickering, D. J. (2008). *Etkili sınıf yönetimi stratejileri* (Çev. Ed. Ç. Turgul). İstanbul: SEV Yayıncılık.

McCauley-Cate, J. (2003). *"This inner-city thing": New teachers and classroom management* (Order No. 3103230). Available from ProQuest Dissertations & Theses Global. (305343725).

Miller, A. (2016). *Tools for student self-management*. USA: George Lucas Educational Foundation.

National Center for Intensive Intervention. (2015). Implementing behavioral strategies. Retrieved from: https://intensiveintervention.org/sites/default/files/Intermittent_Reinforcement_508.pdf

Pellegrino, A. (2010). Pre-service teachers and classroom authority. *American Secondary Education*, *35*(3), 62–78.

Ralph, M. (2019). *Creating space for collaboration*. USA: George Lucas Educational Foundation.

Reis, A. T. (2018). Study on the Alpha Generation and the reflections of its behavior in the organizational environment. *Quest Journals Journal of Research in Humanities and Social Science*, *6*(1), 9–19.

Ritter, J. T., & Hancock, D. R. (2007). Exploring the relationship between certification sources, experience levels, and classroom management orientations of classroom teachers. *Teaching & Teacher Education*, *23*(1), 1206–1216.

Terada, Y. (2018). *Dos and don'ts of classroom decoration*. USA: George Lucas Educational Foundation.

Vijayan, P., Chakravarthi, S., & Philips, J. A. (2016). The role of teachers' behavior and strategies in managing a classroom environment. *International Journal of Social Science and Humanity*, *6*(3), 208–215.

Gürsu Aşık

Measurement and Evaluation in Alpha Classes

Abstract: Depending on the development of technology and innovation, changing expectations are reflected in education systems as serious reform movements. We step into a digital learning era where access enables personalized content. Based on the findings of scientific research for the new era, it is necessary to change and improve education systems, and to reach the goal of innovative education requires alternative measurement and evaluation methods. Generation Alpha, defined as individuals born into technology, have more power to access almost all kinds of content and information than other generations. Digital learning based on technology and personalized content are of utmost importance in the education that is taken by Generation Alpha individuals. At the same time, the education enables individuals to design their own self-learning systems. These students are able to personalize all the technologies they integrate into their lives and put technology at the center more than all other generations. Therefore, online measurement and evaluation methods are at the forefront to monitor the development of individuals as a reflection of the change in the education system. In the new age, where access to scientific information is no longer a problem, it becomes more important to perceive concepts and to establish relationships between concepts than knowledge itself in education. The ability to use basic knowledge and skills acquired by individuals in real life by relating them to their own characteristics will be defined as successful human character. Accordingly, measurement and evaluation has further evolved into formative and holistic assessment processes such as performance task and project work that contributes to the development of higher-order thinking skills such as creativity, critical thinking, collaboration, and communication skills. To summarize, this chapter focused on measurement and evaluation methods for Generation Alpha and aimed to enrich teachers' skills about integrating innovative assessment procedures in the classroom.

Keywords: Generation Alpha, measurement, evaluation, differentiated assessment

With the change in the expectations from social life and society, and with the advancement of innovation and technology, the living conditions of the era are changing, and there is a need to come up with new categorizations for the generations that are defined as "human communities living under similar conditions in the same period". Today's most recent generation, which is comprised of children born after the year 2011 as well as those that are school age, is called Generation Alpha. Each new generation comes up with their own desires and demands, depending on the expectations and needs of the society. These demands and needs must also be met by the reforms to be made in education as well as by the social community and human life.

The most outstanding characteristic of Generation Alpha is that the children of this generation were born into technology. It is inevitable that technology, internet and virtual reality will be a part of their lives as ordinary elements of living. In accordance with the developments in technology and innovation, changing expectations are reflected in education systems as serious reform movements. We are stepping into a digital learning era, where access enables personalized content. Based on findings and projections concerning the new generation, it is necessary to change and improve education systems to a level that appeals to Generation Alpha.

Improving educational programs requires making changes on the tasks, processes and individuals within the system. At this point, one of the transformations necessary to convert the education system to a format that is more appealing to Generation Alpha is to make changes in the measurement and evaluation practices, which is one of the most important components of educational systems. Measurement and evaluation primarily determines whether the instruction delivered has achieved its purpose. It helps to see whether students have learned what they really wanted to learn and whether we really can teach what we are trying to teach. At the same time, measurement and evaluation affect future decisions for professional and career development of individuals. In this context, depending on the changes occurring in generations and societies, it is important that measurement and evaluation keep up with the needs of society as well as individuals in that society.

Measurement refers to quantification of any attribute in any field. It is the process of attaining numerical description – by using systematic rules – of the degree to which an individual possesses a given behavior or performance. In terms of learning, it can be defined as quantification of how much a learner has learned. As a concept closely linked to measurement, assessment is a more commonly used term in education. It is defined as the process of gathering and organizing information for evaluation. The word "assess" originates from the Latin verb "assidere" which means "to sit with" (Green, 1998). It implies that teachers carry out the teaching and learning process together with students. Finally, evaluation is defined as the process of making judgments on the "value" of a performance in accordance with expectations and purposes.

One fact that should not be overlooked at this point is that if we do not measure something properly, we cannot evaluate it correctly. Considering that Generation Alpha will be educated longer and are more knowledgeable than the previous generations, much more reliable measurement tools are needed for this new generation. Integrating technology into measurement processes will assist evaluators in making more consistent and precise measurements.

What to Measure in Alpha Classes

Given the importance of measurement and evaluation for Generation Alpha, one of the questions that comes to mind is what we will measure in the new age. In the new age, accessing scientific information and knowledge is no longer a problem for children. Alpha children will have more power to access almost all kinds of content and information than other generations. Thus, it is more important in education to perceive concepts and establish relationships between them than knowledge itself. The ability to use basic knowledge and skills in real life by harmonizing them with one's own characteristics is the current definition of a successful learner.

We never try to measure a thing or an individual alone. What we measure is always the quality or attribute of this object or person (Thorndike & Thorndike-Christ., 2014). Whether the attributes of an object or person are desirable may vary according to the expectations of the existing environment and society. At this point, the expectations of individuals raised in Generation Alpha cannot be expected to be the same as those raised in previous generations. When the data from country policies, scientific research and applications are examined; cognitive skills such as critical and analytical thinking, creativity, problem-solving and learning to learn, as well as social and emotional skills such as empathy, collaboration and communication come to the forefront as the fundamental skills that individuals should possess in Generation Alpha (Lamb, Maire, & Doecke, 2017; OECD, 2018). Accordingly, measurement and evaluation will further evolve into formative and holistic assessment processes such as performance task and project work, which contribute to the development of higher-order thinking skills such as creativity, critical thinking, collaboration, and communication skills.

Most of the existing evaluation systems have focused on academic knowledge, recall of given information and application of formula-based procedures that are taught. They are more uniformed in nature and reflect the projection of the current situation that is worked on. Given the expectations of Generation Alpha such as critical thinking, communication, collaboration, and creativity, existing systems remain insufficient to meet the need. At this point, educators who are to address the needs of Generation Alpha are expected to focus on measurement of such skills as analytical thinking and performing complex operations rather than having simple knowledge. If the aim of assessment is to improve learning and teaching processes, it is necessary to provide useful and reliable sources of assessment and evaluation that will more clearly demonstrate what students have learned and how they achieve educational goals (Schoenfeld, 2017).

In addition to the basic skills mentioned above, "literacy" is another ability that is emphasized in different contents in the reports written on the 21st-century skills (Fadel, 2008; OECD, 2018). Literacy skills are emphasized as the skills that new generation individuals should possess in different disciplines such as finance, technology, citizenship, informatics, data, media and information. The skill should be measured and evaluated to see both how much it develops in individuals and for the effectiveness of the programs implemented in this context. At this point, "scientific literacy" – as a general term – emerges as a fact that should be included in the context of measurement and evaluation studies.

Individuals with scientific literacy can easily make sense of scientific and technological words and terms, use concepts and meanings in their processes. Moreover, they have not only limited understanding but also narrow perspectives of the role of science and technology in personal life and society (Holbrook & Rannikmae, 2009). Given that Generation Alpha individuals can easily access all kinds of information, it is primarily expected that individuals are able to understand, interpret, and use these pieces of information effectively. This requires individuals to have scientific literacy. Expectations in society and working life require a transformation to meet expectations in education systems. This transformation can also be reflected in the measurement and evaluation process, which is an important part of the education system. Thus, scientific literacy is going to take its place in educational systems ever-increasingly as an important attribute that should be measured.

In addition to scientific literacy, another literacy skill that should be particularly emphasized for Generation Alpha is technology literacy. The idea behind technological literacy is that individuals can work more effectively if they have a basic understanding of technology in a world where technology is permeated. Technology literacy does not mean knowing how each new technology works, its advantages and disadvantages, and how to use it. Nevertheless, an individual who is technologically literate can easily obtain enough information to decide whether or not s/he can use or prefer not to use a product when s/he deems it necessary. A higher level of technological literacy will always benefit individuals and society as a whole.

Technology literacy stands out as a requirement for educators who address Generation Alpha as well as for students. Teachers should also be technology literate in order to use technology effectively and find technology-based applications that meet their needs. In a study conducted with 970 teachers in the United States in 2013, 92 % of teachers stated that educational technology

(EdTech) tools should be used in classrooms, but only 14 % of the participants stated that they integrated these tools into their own curriculum (Common Sense Media, 2013). The results show that the use of educational technology in classes is not optional, but rather an essential component of the process. The need for technological literacy is greater than ever. Soon, teachers will find it necessary to increase technology literacy in order to increase their relationship with alphabets and to make their teaching more effective.

How to Measure in Alpha Classes

The most fundamental characteristic that distinguishes Generation Alpha children from those of other generations is that they were born into the center of technology and the virtual world. These students are able to personalize all the technologies they integrate into their lives and put technology at the center more than all other generations did. Digital learning, based on technology and personalized content, is of utmost importance in the education that is taken by Generation Alpha. It is irrelevant to subject those children born and raised in this generation to classical assessment strategies, such as traditional pen and paper tests. Even the oldest members of Generation Alpha children have not yet reached age 10; when we look at the measurement and evaluation practices in today's world, it is seen that the number of technology-enabled measurement tools for measurement in education is increasing with each passing day. When we examine online stores for apps and similar content, it is possible to see many digital measurement tools and applications that measure different knowledge and skills in different disciplines. The number of such applications suitable for many different contents is going to increase gradually.

In addition to the quantitative increase in the number of digital measurement tools for different needs, the qualitative characteristics of how and how well they perform the measurement are also important. In this context, single-acting measurement tools, whose content is set beforehand – and therefore cannot be manipulated – cannot be expected to adapt to the needs of the new generation. At this point, digital measurement tools will evolve into measurement systems where different measurement tools are harmonious. The development of digital measurement and evaluation platforms built as an integrated system will benefit from data access with precise measurements, data processing and provide reliable and detailed information for the evaluators to generate even greater insight.

Digital measurement and evaluation platforms to be developed for the new generation must meet certain criteria. Structurally, such platforms need to be up-to-date and rich in content. It is expected to be flexible and modular for users with different personality traits, and to offer teachers the opportunity to add their own content. Similarly, it should provide detailed reporting opportunities for both teachers and students for assessment and evaluation. Finally, all users can be expected to have cloud-based access to the platforms independent of time and space. This way, users will be able to connect to the system at any time and place using a variety of options such as computers, mobile applications and tablets.

It goes without saying that technology-based assessments are rapidly increasing in information–communication technology (ICT) applications which are growing steadily at all levels of education (Csapó, Ainley, Bennett, Latour, & Law, 2012). Technology applications offer new assessment methods that traditional forms cannot perform, and also many traditional assessment processes used today can be performed more efficiently and effectively with computers. In addition to enabling the assessment to be carried out in a shorter period of time, it also helps to provide instant feedback to students. The use of technology is also more appealing to Generation Alpha. Technology-based digital assessments will undoubtedly replace pen and paper tests that stand out in most traditional assessment scenarios. Technology-assisted assessment methods, on the other hand, will expand their use in different areas of education as they enable individuals to provide more frequent and precise feedback.

Although there are many digital measurement and evaluation tools available today, the number of these tools is rapidly increasing. When the basic characteristics of these instruments are examined, it is seen that they give autonomy to students, encourage collaboration and group work and facilitate communication between teachers and students. It is seen that many digital platforms are designed not only for evaluation but also as integrated systems to support the learning and teaching process.

When we consider technology-assisted learning tools for Generation Alpha, the most comprehensive digital tools are learning platforms that focus on both teaching and measurement. These platforms offer different content for every age group, from preschool to university. Learning platforms include easy-to-use features and different measurement tools for each subject. The content can be pre-written according to the curriculum by educators who are experts in their fields, or it can be manipulated by the teacher. Learning platforms are educational tools that connect teachers and students and resemble a social network. On interactive learning platforms, teachers can create collaborative groups online, manage and provide educational materials, measure student performance, and communicate with parents. They are also management systems that allow teachers to create exercises or educational games that students can reach using mobile devices such as smartphones, laptops or tablets. Teachers can see the results of the assessment activities instantly at any time and adjust future classes to make the learning process more personal.

In addition to the educational platforms where learning, teaching and assessment processes are integrated, the number of more subject-oriented digital assessment tools is increasing day by day. It can be said that the most frequently used tools of this type are the applications that allow the preparation of quizzes and tests in different visuals and frames. With these tools, different types of multiple-choice, open-ended, and visually interactive questions can be prepared. One of the biggest advantages of digital quizzes and tests is that they can be used to give instant feedback to students and even the results can be projected and discussed in class. Thus, it can be used as a formative assessment tool. Another benefit is that most digital quizzes and test applications are also game-based tools. In this way, by creating a dynamic, fun, and social environment for education, these tools increase the participation of the students and encourage game-based learning.

Besides traditional assessment tools such as pen and paper tests and exams, the number of digital tools for alternative assessment is increasing nowadays. Alternative assessment is also called performance tests or authentic assessment. It is a form of student performance rating that provides a more holistic approach to student assessment and focuses on measuring proficiency rather than knowledge. To reach the goal of innovative education requires alternative measurement and evaluation methods.

A teacher using alternative assessment tools may ask students to perform their ability in different ways. Teachers may create or ask students to create multimedia presentations with dynamic slides in which they can embed text, pictures, music, videos, interactive maps, and online quizzes to this presentation. Teachers may also ask students to create digital concept maps, digital posters and bulletin boards, websites, cartoons, animated videos, and interactive story books with the appropriate digital assessment tools. And even though augmented reality applications have started to be used as teaching material in classes, they will soon be used more by teachers as an alternative assessment tool. Educational end-products demanded by the teacher will be prepared in technology-supported environments, which will increase student learning motivation and make the information learned more memorable.

Differentiated Assessment in Alpha Classes

It is predicted that Alpha students who are instructed differently from past generations will be able to understand their world and use the skills they have. In this context, the evaluation of Alpha students cannot be expected to be held in one-size-fits-all classrooms. In the near future, each individual will be subjected to differentiated assessments to suit his or her personality. The assessment also needs to be differentiated to ensure harmony between the curriculum, instruction, and the assessment to be performed.

Differentiated assessment can be defined as teachers' use of different assessment methods for the same purpose in line with the characteristics of students. Students differ in their previous learning experiences, learning styles, preferences, academic positions, abilities, strengths and weaknesses, and culture and backgrounds. Designing various assessments that are appropriate for specific groups of students provides more opportunities for students to demonstrate what they have learned in ways that are appropriate and effective for them. Differentiated assessment also guides teachers in how they can distinguish, change, and improve their own teaching. In order to make differentiated assessment, teachers should have knowledge and experience of alternative measurement methods and tools.

Self-Assessment

Generation Alpha is more fortunate in terms of accessing the information than other generations, and have the ability to personalize all the technologies that they own and integrate into their lives, resulting in the individualization of learning processes. Personalized learning offers a more holistic and person-centered approach to learner development. Personalizing something requires that it be meaningful and engaging for the individual. Personalization in the learning process will also pave the way for the use of methods and tools for self-assessment. In this respect, as the importance of self-assessment will increase in the education of Alpha students, technology-assisted assessment tools such as digital self-reflection forms will play a more important role in educational systems.

In the process of self-assessment of individuals, the first step for teachers should be to determine learning objectives on their own or together with students. Then there should be a joint plan with the students to test how many of these learning objectives have been achieved. Individuals will be able to evaluate themselves easily as they will know the expectations of their teachers and curriculum. In this way, individuals will be able to identify deficiencies in knowledge and skills, monitor their progress, set more realistic goals for themselves, and decide when to move to the next level in their online training. Self-evaluation of individuals will also help individuals design their own learning systems.

Closing Remarks

The characteristics of the Alpha individuals and the fact that technology will be more crucial in education than ever will bring many innovations and expectations in terms of what to measure and how to measure in Generation Alpha. Accordingly, measurement processes are expected to have a more personalized and technology-supported manner. Although there are innovations in measurement systems, we, as teachers and educators, are responsible for the evaluation part. Evaluation is the process of making decisions about the "value" of an individual's performance and attributes. Thus, teachers are the ones to decide how good, sufficient, and desirable the performance and attribute is. Although Alpha students are the main reason for the need for change in education and assessment, teachers and educators of the past generation need to adapt to the new expectations in order to achieve this change in a healthy way. Easy adaptation to such and similar changes may also be considered as part of the definition of being a good educator.

References

Casner-Lotto, J., & Barrington, L. (2006). *Are they really ready to work? Employers' perspectives on the basic knowledge and applied skills of new entrants to the 21st century US workforce*. Partnership for 21st Century Skills, Washington, DC.

Common Sense Media. (2013). *Teaching with technology: The promise and reality of the U.S. digital classroom*. Retrieved from: https://www.commonsense.org/education/sites/default/files/tlr-blog/teachingwithtechnology-thepromiseandrealityoftheusdigitalclassroom.pdf

Csapó, B., Ainley, J., Bennett, R. E., Latour, T., & Law, N. (2012). Technological issues for computer-based assessment. In *Assessment and teaching of 21st century skills* (pp. 143–230). Dordrecht: Springer.

Fadel, C. (2008). 21st Century Skills: How can you prepare students for the new Global Economy? Retrieved February, 20, 2018.

Green, J. M. (1998, February). Constructing the way forward for all students. A Speech Delivered at "Innovations for Effective Schools" OECD/New Zealand Joint Follow-Up Conference, Christchurch, New Zealand.

Holbrook, J., & Rannikmae, M. (2009). The meaning of scientific literacy. *International Journal of Environmental and Science Education*, *4*(3), 275–288.

Lamb, S., Maire, Q., & Doecke, E. (2017). *Key skills for the 21st Century: An evidence-based review*. Retrieved from: https://education.nsw.gov.au/our-priorities/innovate-for-the-future/education-for-a-changing-world/

researchfindings/future-frontiers-analytical-report-key-skills-for-the-21st-century/Key-Skills-for-the-21st-Century-AnalyticalReport.pdf

OECD. (2018). *The future of education and skills: Education 2030*. Retrieved from: http://www.oecd.org/education/2030/E2030 %20Position%20 Paper%20(05.04.2018).pdf

Schoenfeld, A. H. (2017). On learning and assessment. *Assessment in Education: Principles, Policy, & Practice*, *24*, 369–378.

Thorndike, R. M., & Thorndike-Christ, T. M. (2014). *Measurement and evaluation in psychology and education* (8th ed.). USA: Pearson.

Hülya Avcı and Tufan Adıgüzel

Leveraging Digital Intelligence in Generation Alpha

Abstract: In today's world, there has been a growing proclivity in promoting and teaching digital skills, which are more crucial than ever before, considering the world transformed by technology. In parallel with it, the term "Digital Intelligence (DQ)" has gained a global recognition as we enter the age of digital transformation. In a simple definition, DQ is associated with our interactions with technology; more specifically, it is the aggregate of social, emotional, and cognitive abilities that foster individuals to adapt emotions and adjust behaviors and credentials to cope with the digital life. Regarding the DQ framework, digital citizenship is the core competency necessary to be accomplished in a global job market. Digital citizenship encompasses an array of skills, which are branched out into eight macro competencies: (a) digital citizen identity, (b) screen time management, (c) privacy management, (d) cyberbullying management, (e) cybersecurity management, (f) critical thinking, (g) digital footprints, and (h) digital empathy. The challenge for teachers is to come up with effective strategies to equip Generation Alpha, who can gain independent access to the Internet, with these skills. Hence, this chapter purports to guide teachers on how to enhance the DQ digital citizenship abilities of Generation Alpha and ensure they have these skills to satisfy the needs and challenges of the digital world.

Keywords: Generation Alpha, digital intelligence, digital citizenship, DQ skills

The digital revolution has generated profound changes in the information technology (IT) area in the last five decades. The role and relevance of IT in the digital universe have become indispensable in every aspect of our lives today, considering a myriad of innovations and technologies getting clutched to the whole world. As digital intelligence (DQ) facilitates grasping and employing the potential of IT to our benefit rather than solely helping access information, DQ has become one of the core skills of business and IT managers in today's economy (Mithas, 2016). Not only the business entities but also the educational settings have been rapidly undergoing changes due to interaction with digital technologies, thereby demanding people who can perform effectively, possess technical and professional expertise to orchestrate projects, and confront any challenges with confidence and collaborative work in a digital era.

In education, Multiple Intelligence (MI) Theory developed by Gardner (1983, 1993) has guided teaching and learning, and extensively influenced teaching practices around the world. The theoretical framework of Multiple Intelligences can enable to embrace and settle a new concept that a new "digital intelligence" has surfaced (Adams, 2011). Acknowledgment of the notion of digital intelligence might lead the improvement of a novel intellectual style in educational practices as Gardner (2009) evidently already beholds that "the world of the future - with its ubiquitous search engines, robots, and other computational devices - will demand capacities that until now have been mere options. To meet this new world on its own terms, we should begin to cultivate these capacities now" (p. 2).

It obviously appears that the need of understanding the concept of digital intelligence and utilizing it effectively for instructional purposes is critical. However, there is little or no empirical data available to truly evaluate the demands of Generation Alpha. Given the deficiency and underdevelopment of Generation Alpha's theoretical explanations for the development of digital competencies, we can suggest some guidelines for the teachers of Generation Alpha on how to enhance their students' digital competencies with more emphasis on digital citizenship. In the next section, we provide some definitions of the term "digital intelligence" requisite for understanding the chapter.

Definition of Digital Intelligence

After coining the terms "digital natives" and "digital immigrants" in his article in 2001, Prensky (2009) introduced the concept "digital wisdom" as a twofold term, pertaining both to "wisdom arising from the use of digital technology to access cognitive power beyond our innate capacity and to wisdom in the prudent use of technology to enhance our capabilities" (p. 3) while we use the term "digital intelligence" (Echenique, 2014) and the acronym "DQ" which was coined by the DQ institute in 2016. According to Prensky (2009), technology itself is not adequate to equip individuals with the mindset of benefiting from all resources of digital technology by distilling these resources to find what they need, thus demanding a digital wisdom to improve their intuition, problem-solving and critical-thinking skills. At the World Economic Forum (WEF), Park (2016), who is the founder of DQ Institute, underlined the concept "digital intelligence" which is grounded on the theory of Gardner (1983). According to the 2019 DQ Global Standards Report (DQGSR), DQ has been described as an umbrella concept for orchestrating "digital skills," "digital literacy," and "digital readiness" among various sectors and communities. Recently, Park (2019) rephrases DQ as "a comprehensive set of technical, cognitive, meta-cognitive, and socio-emotional competencies grounded in universal moral values that enable individuals to face the challenges of digital life and adapt to its demands" (p. 13). These abilities (Fig. 1) are divided into eight broad areas (DQGSR, 2019, p. 14) as follows:

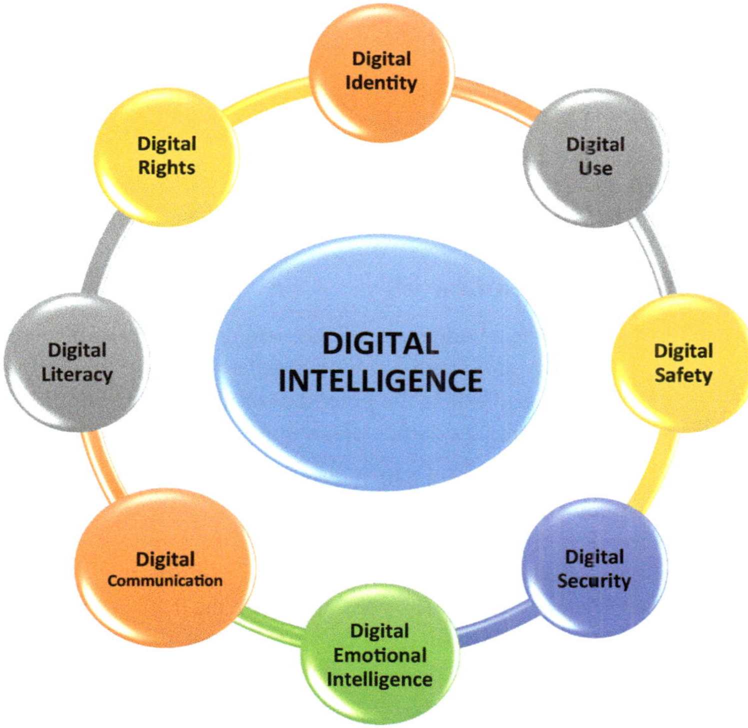

Fig. 1: Eight Areas of DQ

I. "Digital Identity: The ability to build a wholesome online and offline identity.
II. Digital Use: The ability to use technology in a balanced, healthy, and civic way.
III. Digital Safety: The ability to understand, mitigate, and manage various cyber-risks through safe, responsible, and ethical use of technology.
IV. Digital Security: The ability to detect, avoid, and manage different levels of cyber threats to protect data, devices, networks, and systems.
V. Digital Emotional Intelligence: The ability to recognize, navigate, and express emotions in one's intra and inter-personal interactions.
VI. Digital Communication: The ability to communicate and collaborate with others using technology.
VII. Digital Literacy: The ability to find, read, evaluate, synthesize, create, adapt, and share info, media, and technology.

VIII. Digital Rights: The ability to understand and uphold human rights when using technology."

As a result, individuals having DQ abilities become smart, qualified, and potential digital citizens who are capable of using, managing, and generating technology to leverage humanity (Park, 2019). Furthermore, these DQ competencies have been recognized as crucial for our advancing universe by the OECD (2018), the WEF (2018), the World Bank (2019), and the United Nations (2018).

Digital Intelligence Framework

Digital Intelligence refers to a wide range of competencies comprising technical, cognitive, meta-cognitive, and socio-emotional skills that allow individuals to confront with difficulties and utilize the potentials of digital world (Park, 2016). The DQ Framework has three fundamental features (Park, 2019) as follows:

a. "*all-embracing concept*" (p. 12) which provides the aggregation of digital skills, digital literacy, and digital readiness across different fields and societies.
b. "*adaptable framework*" (p. 13) which is a reference framework enabling a holistic structure of digital skills with a systematic pattern, thus offering any schools, organizations, and institutions to adopt the DQ Framework and easily adjust it in deference to their needs.
c. "*agile evolution*" (p. 13) which refers to constantly compiles information and practices from around the world to provide pedagogically and technically contemporary framework.

The DQ Framework is categorized into two dimensions including "areas" and "levels." The identified eight areas of DQ competencies can be further distinguished by three "levels" of maturity consisting of digital citizenship, digital creativity, and digital competitiveness, thus supporting individuals' learning considering their current digital life. According to the recent report by the DQ Institute (DQGSR, 2019), each of these DQ competences well corresponds to the OECD Education 2030 Learning Framework, the UN Sustainable Development Goals (SDGs), Universal Declaration of Human Rights, and the OECD Well-Being Indicators.

In this chapter, we focus on the DQ level of "*digital citizenship*" enabling a broad array of essential digital skills (Fig. 2) since currently Generation Alpha students might be highly exposed to misapplication of technology (Miles, 2011). Thus, they are likely to experience certain emotional and psychological distress including "their perceived anonymity, their accumulated digital portfolio or digital footprint, and the legal implications of thoughtless or malicious actions"

Fig. 2: Digital Citizenship

(Oxley, 2011, p. 2). One solution to deal with this cyber safety trouble is digital citizenship. There are multiple definitions and explanations as to what actually digital citizenship is. First, digital citizenship is identified as "the ability to use digital technology and media in safe, responsible, and ethical ways" (Park, 2019, p. 15). With its generic definition, digital citizenship signifies "being able to find, access, use and create information effectively; to engage with other users and with content in an active, critical, sensitive and ethical manner; and navigate the online and ICT environment safely and responsibly while being aware of one's own rights" (Tan et al., 2016, p. 125). The International Society for Technology in Education (ISTE) establishes Digital Citizenship standards for students, broadly delineating "digital citizens" as students who (a) develop and manage their digital identity and are cognizant of the durability of their actions in the digital platforms; (b) practice safe, legal, and ethical use of technology and information;

(c) exhibit consideration and respect for the rights of sharing and using information; and (d) demonstrate individual responsibility to manage their digital privacy and security and are conscious of their online actions being tracked by data-collection tools (ISTE, 2016). More specifically, eight skills of digital citizenship (Park, 2019, p. 16) are indicated as follows:

I. "Digital Citizen Identity: The ability to set up and manage a healthy identity online and offline.
II. Screen Time Management: The ability to manage screen time, multitasking, and engagement online with self-control.
III. Cyberbullying Management: The ability to detect cyber-bullying situations and handle them wisely.
IV. Cyber Security Management: The ability to protect one's data by creating strong passwords and manage cyber-attacks.
V. Privacy Management: The ability to handle with discretion all personal information shared online to protect privacy.
VI. Critical Thinking: The ability to distinguish between true and false information, good and harmful content, and trustworthy and questionable contacts online.
VII. Digital Footprints: The ability to understand the nature of digital footprints and their real-life consequences and to manage them responsibly.
VIII. Digital Empathy: The ability to be empathetic towards one's and others' needs and feelings online."

The framework of digital citizenship adopts a child-centered approach aligned with the human rights of children (Tan et al., 2016); this has been underscored in many global platforms, including the United Nations Committee on the Rights of the Child, in a report by Mendel (2015), in the Internet Governance Forum (2017), and in the Council of Europe (2016).

Enhancing Digital Intelligence Skills of Generation Alpha

The world abounds that as technology drastically changes our lives, we need to struggle to keep up with changes, and another perspective is "each generation will become more digital than the preceding one" (Negroponte, 1995, p. 231). However, it could be far beyond our capability of perception and control. The underlying causes of these common conceptions are usually based on the notion that developments in technology necessitate novel approaches and practices in modern life, particularly, in education. Regarding the various descriptions of generations of learners such as baby boomers, Generation X, Generation, Y, etc., we aim to center upon another new kind of learner, Generation Alpha, and discuss some implications in relation with digital intelligence.

One broad argument is that Generation Alpha is different from other generations as their thinking and learning style are distinct owing to their unceasing exposure to digital technology. Reviewing the various claims and debates over the technology experiences of Generation Alpha, it seems there are plenty of concerns about shortage of social interactions, cyberbullying, and technology addiction (e.g., Cross et al., 2009); however, on the other hand, there are promising expectations from this highly technology-driven generation (e.g., Lorenzo et al., 2007).

According to the 2018 DQ Impact Report, over half of 38,000 children aged 8–12 across 29 countries were exposed to at least one of cyber-risks such as cyberbullying, excessive screen time, video game addiction, online privacy mismanagement, offline meetings, digital identity theft, and online sexual behavior (DQ Institute, 2018). Therefore, this raises some critical issues concerning the needs and technology use of young people both in formal and informal educational contexts. Regarding the urgency of setting up norms for improving digital skills of individuals, DQ Institute Founder, Dr. Yuhyun Park and Professor of Psychology at Iowa State University, Dr. Douglas Gentile respectively state as follows:

> "Companies, governments and organizations invest millions each year in developing digital literacy and skills, yet there is a severe lack of coordination or a globally shared understanding of what terms like digital skills and digital literacy mean, and it is difficult to address how to improve and sustain them. For the world to build comprehensive digital competency more efficiently and effectively, there is an urgent need for coordination and consensus on a common set of understanding, structure and taxonomy — a global standard for digital literacy, skills, and readiness…" (DQGSR, 2019)
>
> "We have been talking about digital literacy in the U.S. since the 1980s. Unfortunately, we haven't made much progress, partly because we don't have a common framework. When we say digital literacy a lot of people just think of computer skills. Others may think about media violence or even computer programming. All are a part of digital literacy, but there hasn't been a framework to integrate all these pieces. With proper digital literacy education, we reduce the risks children face and give them the skills they'll need to be successful in a new economy." (DQGSR, 2019)

It is evident that a lack of common framework for digital competencies among young people poses a high challenge for schools, industries, and nations. Another report on "digital skills crisis" by the UK Science and Technology Committee of the House of Commons (2016) revealed that over 12.6 million of the adult population in the UK are deprived of basic digital skills, and around 5.8 million people have never used the internet; thus resulting in a serious digital skills gap which further leads to an estimated £63 billion a year in lost GDP. Furthermore, the development of emerging technologies generates a pressing demand for high-level digital competencies in such fields as cyber security, data analytics, data security, and mobile computing in our changing world.

In the face of this inadequacy, teaching and promoting digital competencies such as digital literacy, digital skills, and digital readiness have become fundamental for seeking job opportunities of Generation Alpha and deploying workforce with the right set of skills and knowledge. Given that, we strongly believe in the future, one of the responsibilities of schools will be to contribute students' digital intelligence to easily adapt to changes resulting from continuous innovations in technology, and become prepared to successfully handle any potential technological threats. Additionally, considering that during their pre-service training, teachers of Generation Alpha have not obtained instruction on how to teach digital competencies, we need DQ-enhanced schools which are able to supply with appropriate digital materials and training for teachers to enrich their practices with DQ-based activities in the classroom. Hence, first of all, a DQ-oriented course including digital competencies such as digital safety, digital empathy, and digital footprints should be embedded in the school curriculum rather than only the technical skills.

To leverage the digital skills of Generation Alpha, we can recommend educators and schools to integrate the DQ Framework into their teaching practices. In essence, our purpose is to guide the teachers of Generation Alpha to aid them gain a deep understanding of DQ and to bring the digital citizenship education to every child, bridging the gaps in education systems that do not still have sufficient resources or expertise to provide their citizens with these essential skills. Alderman Peter Estlin, the Lord Mayor for the City of London, has proposed an outline of his digital skills strategy, which is grounded on the DQ Framework and emphasized its significance as follows:

> "The concept of DQ provides a universal standard from which a more comprehensive understanding of the need for digital skills can be developed. This allowed us to build on existing initiatives and set out the actions we need to take. As a framework, DQ provides a basis for measurement and comparison, in the same way as IQ has been used until now." (DQGSR, 2019)

According to the Digital Citizenship standards for teachers proposed by ISTE (2016), teachers are expected to:

- Show awareness of regional and global social issues and duties in a growing digital culture and behave legally and ethically in their professional practice.

- Teach, model, and support using digital information by taking account of legal, safe, and ethical matters, including respect for copyright, proper documentation of sources, and so on.
- Fulfill the various needs of all students by utilizing students-focused approaches, enabling equal access to suitable digital tools and resources.
- Encourage and model digital etiquette and amenable social communication on using technology and information.
- Gain and model cultural understanding and awareness through interactions with teachers and students from other countries using the digital-age communication and collaboration means.

Another study by Ribble and Bailey (2007) focused on nine core elements of digital citizenship briefly consisting of access, commerce, communication, literacy, etiquette, law, rights and responsibilities, health and wellness, and security. As each element comprises relevant components of current technology use related to student learning and academic performance, student behavior and environment, and student after-school life, it has been employed by schools as a reference while setting up their curriculum. Regarding our purpose, though there is no step-by-step structure for implementing the DQ framework and dealing with teaching digital citizenship at schools, we can suggest stakeholders in education the following strategies of digital citizenship to develop and implement:

a. Offering a DQ-oriented course

Educational institutions can set up a blended compulsory course for Generation Alpha to improve their digital citizenship, which is teem with a set of digital skills for individuals' digital daily life and professional careers. The key issue is the would-be program or course for promoting digital citizenship that should be adaptable and take into account the needs of this Generation Alpha. As a suggestion, a DQ-oriented course could be provided with its integration into the instruction of digital literacy aligning the DQ Framework with the characteristics of Generation Alpha, thus ensuring a deeper understanding and effective implementation of DQ, which will address the needs of Generation Alpha. It should also be noted that schools might need a special program to upskill teachers who are not yet prepared for teaching more advanced digital competencies.

b. Upskilling teachers

The context of digital citizenship can be incorporated as part of teacher competency standards in equipping them with more comprehensive DQ skills to teach students the use of digital technology in a safe, ethical, and responsible manner underlining the backbones of digital citizenship. In addition, educational policy-makers should consider the changing trends of technology and accordingly ensure that teachers have prerequisite ICT knowledge and skills to effectively conduct the affordances of ICT in the classroom settings.

c. Informal learning

The new generation of Generation Alpha can develop a deeper comprehension and mastery of digital competencies through informal learning, outside the curriculum. For instance, free volunteer-led after-school activities including the design of video games, animations, and websites could be conducted under the guidance of teachers to boost digital citizenship skills of Generation Alpha.

d. Improving critical thinking

The development of critical-thinking capacity is a core skill grounding digital citizenship, thus requiring learners to enhance their critical and analytical thinking to become aware of the threats of disinformation and misinformation, and to independently manage their security and safety in digital platforms. Regarding that, teachers should create learning environments including activities that encourage students to identify and analyze problems and then come up with solutions to discuss and evaluate each in a collaborative fashion. Besides having critical-thinking ability, students should be able to look through problems from multiple perspectives, which contributes to their problem-solving skills.

What Should Teachers of Generation Alpha Do?

Integrate DQ

The most significant aspect might be the inclusion of DQ at the primary and secondary level of basic schools. Taking into consideration that students are exposed to cyber threats at an early age and tend to misuse technology and commit cybercrimes such as digital cheating without realizing the outcomes of their actions, first teachers need to support the necessity of implementation of DQ at schools as early as possible.

Optimize Teaching Contents

The teaching content within the overall curriculum can be properly divided into sub-units including core topics (e.g., digital identity, digital rights, etc.) of digital intelligence. Through the interdisciplinary relations between digital literacy and digital citizenship, thematic integrated units can be generated under one teaching subject. As an example, teachers can incorporate lesson plans guiding students towards the safe, ethical, and responsible use of online sources, thus helping them capture the mindset of when to trust or not trust an online source while navigating online platforms.

Elaborate Learning Activities

Teachers need to seek for multiple ways of reinforcing their lessons with competencies identified as digital citizenship. As active learning requires more efficient learning strategies, informal learning activities can be encouraged more to increase digital skills of students. For instance, teachers can launch collaborations with other schools to apply and participate in out-of-school activities such as designing clubs for coding, video games, etc. As mentioned, activities supporting analytical and critical thinking can help students take responsibility of their decisions on which might be best for their needs and purposes while utilizing digital technologies. Thus, commitment of teachers as role models in a school setting can significantly influence students' stage of digital skills.

Hone Digital Skills

Teachers of Generation Alpha are not only liable to equip their students with skills necessary to survive in the digital world, but also take ownership of enhancing their own digital competencies to be able to meet the changing needs of their students who are becoming the most technologically literate generation. Therefore, teachers should develop and adapt their abilities and efforts to learn different approaches that can facilitate them to gain the qualifications and confidence to teach advanced digital skills in conjunction with the potential DQ-focused curriculum.

Supply Resources

Although government is primarily responsible to provide schools with key digital resources to establish the optimal conditions for digital intelligence development, teachers can take initiative by first realizing their role in ensuring opportunities for students' equal access to a wide variety of digital learning materials, and then enriching their teaching practices in collaboration with subject-matter experts (SMEs), colleagues, and government.

Conclusion

The growing complexity of modern life requires a deep understanding of knowledge and concepts, besides practical skills, attitudes, and intuitions to overcome challenges in the growing digitized world. Today, young people or so-called Generation Alpha can independently decide and manage multiple digital identities, as a result, demanding more from the digital world to meet their individual needs. Properly established and adaptable digital citizenship curriculum could provide guidance for students who become the members of digital communities. For this reason, we need more schools which are planning to shift from traditional methods of interacting with Generation Alpha to the approaches more convenient for the current and incoming Generation Alpha students. As suggested, the development and implementation of the DQ Framework at schools could enable Generation Alpha to equip themselves with the identified digital competencies, and become ready and eligible to keep pace with the new advances of technology. Therefore, policy-makers, educators, or teachers of Generation Alpha play an important role to provide their students with multiple effective educational opportunities promoting their digital citizenship and overall digital competencies.

References

Adams, N. B. (2011). Digital intelligence: A new way of knowing. In G. Vincenti & J. Braman (Eds.), *Teaching through multi-user virtual environments: Applying dynamic elements to the modern classroom* (pp. 59–65). Hershey, PA: IGI Global.

Council of Europe, Council of Europe Strategy for the Rights of the Child (2016-2021). (2016). Children's human rights. Retrieved from; https://rm.coe.int/168066cff8

Cross, D., Shaw, T., Hearn, L., Epstein, M., Monks, H., Lester, L., & Thomas, L. (2009). *Australian covert bullying prevalence study*. Perth: Child Health Promotion Research Centre, Edith Cowan University. Retrieved from: http://www.deewr.gov.au/Schooling/NationalSafeSchools/ Pages/research.aspx

DQ Institute, DQ Global Standards Report (DQGSR) 2019. (2019). Common *f*ramework for *d*igital *l*iteracy, *s*kills and *r*eadiness. Retrieved from: https://www.dqinstitute.org/wpcontent/uploads/2019/03/DQGlobalStandardsReport2019.pdf

DQ Institute. (2018). DQ Impact Report. Retrieved from: https://www.dqinstitute.org/2018dq_impact_report

Echenique, E. G. (2014). An integrative review of literature on learners in the digital era. *Studia Paedagogica, 19*(4), 161–184.

Gardner, H. (1983). *Frames of mind: The theory of multiple intelligences.* New York: Basic Books.

Gardner, H. (1993). *Multiple intelligences: The theory in practice.* New York: Basic Books.

Gardner, H. (2009). *Multiple intelligences around the world.* New York: Basic Books.

House of Commons, Science and Technology Committee. (2016). Report on Digital Skills Crisis. Retrieved from: https://publications.parliament.uk/pa/cm201617/cmselect/cmsctech/270/270.pdf

International Society for Technology in Education (ISTE). (2016). ISTE Standards for Students. Retrieved from: https://www.iste.org/standards/for-students

Internet Governance Forum (IGF), Summary of IGF 2016 – Abridged Report. (2017). Enabling *i*nclusive and *s*ustainable *g*rowth. Retrieved from: http://www.intgovforum.org/multilingual/filedepot_download/3367/1048

Lorenzo, G., Oblinger, D., & Dziuban, C. (2007). How choice, co-creation, and culture are changing what it means to be net savvy. *Educause Quarterly, 30*, 6–12.

Mendel, T. (2015). The UN Special Rapporteur on freedom of opinion and expression: Progressive development of international standards relating to freedom of expression. In T. McGonagle & Y. Donders (Eds.), The United Nations and *f*reedom of *e*xpression and *i*nformation: Critical *p*erspectives (pp. 235–268). Cambridge: Cambridge University Press. doi:10.1017/CBO9781316018552.009

Miles, D. (2011). Youth protection: Digital citizenship-principles and new resources. Paper presented at *Second Worldwide Cybersecurity Summit (WCS)*, 2011.

Mithas, S. (2016). *Digital intelligence: What every smart manager must have for success in an information age.* North Potomac, MD: Finerplanet.

Negroponte, N. (1995). *Being digital.* New York: Knopf.

Organisation for Economic Co-operation and Development. (2018). The Future of Education and Skills, Education 2030. Retrieved from: https://www.oecd.org/education/2030/E2030 %20Position%20Paper%20(05.04.2018).pdf

Oxley, C. (2011). Digital citizenship: Developing an ethical and responsible online culture. *Access, 25*(3), 5–9.

Park, Y. (2016). 8 Digital Skills We Must Teach Our Children. Retrieved from: https://www.weforum.org/agenda/2016/06/8-digital-skills-we-must-teach-our-children/

Park, Y. (2019). DQ Global Standards Report 2019. Retrieved from: https://www.dqinstitute.org/wpcontent/uploads/2019/03/DQGlobalStandardsReport2019

Prensky, M. (2009). H. sapiens digital: from digital immigrants and digital natives to digital wisdom. *Innovate: Journal of Online Education*, *5*(3), 1–11.

Ribble, M., & Bailey, G. (2007). *Digital citizenship in schools*. Washington, DC: ISTE. ISBN:978-1-56484-232-9.

Tan, M. M., Teng, J. X., & Park, J. (2016). Building digital citizenship in Asia Pacific: A review of policy readiness. In *Proceedings of EdMedia 2016-World Conference on Educational Media and Technology* (pp. 129–142). Vancouver, BC, Canada: Association for the Advancement of Computing in Education (AACE).

United Nations. Sustainable Development Goals. (2018). Retrieved from: https://www.un.org/sustainabledevelopment/sustainable-development-goals/

World Development Report. (2019). The Changing Nature of Work. Retrieved from: http://documents.worldbank.org/curated/en/816281518818814423/2019-WDR-Report.pdf

World Economic Forum. (2018). The Future of Jobs Report. Retrieved from: http://www3.weforum.org/docs/WEF_Future_of_Jobs_2018.pdf

Ergün Akgün

Data Literacy to Understand Generation Alpha

Abstract: This chapter focused on providing data literacy skills for teachers so that they are able to meet the basic requirements of Generation Alpha and the environment they are born into. This environment, called as Education 4.0, is included in education literature with the concept of Industry 4.0 and reflects the importance of decision-making processes. Data literacy can be defined as the analysis of what the data itself mean in the most general sense. To achieve this literacy, some skills such as reading charts and tables, making inferences from data, and even identifying misleading data in deceptive data are required. In order to develop these skills, the following concepts are crucial: a) Awareness: Development of data literacy skills, b) Decision-making: Operation of decision-making mechanisms based on data in decision-making processes, and c) Dissemination: The issues on establishing a microlevel policy in institutions for the institutional dissemination and enhancing the development and implementation phases. Within this framework, this chapter focuses on basic concepts of literacy and provides general information about literacy characteristics and types of literacy in the 21st century. Then, it illuminates skills that are needed to be data literate; types of data that teachers frequently encounter in daily life; creating data sources; and lastly, explain the process of acquiring data literacy skills.

Keywords: Generation Alpha, data literacy, teacher, data literacy skills

Science and technology are rapidly transforming the economy, industry, and education, while at the same speed also transforming human beings themselves. As part of this transformation, new generations have emerged, each with different characteristics. The so-called X, Y, and Z generations have been replaced by Generation Alpha, which has used technology almost since the day its members opened their eyes in this world. It can be said that Generation Alpha, which can adapt to technology and the innovations it brings within a very short period of time, has a unique, inherent ability in terms of using technology. These individuals, who through near constant interaction with technology are exposed to an enormous flow of information, require the competencies necessary to obtain, manage, evaluate, and apply data in ways different from previous generations. Therefore, the education prescribed to Generation Alpha should be planned differently from that of previous generations, such that as individuals and society this generation can move forward.

Today, technology has become an integral part of human life, and – thanks to the widespread use of consumer devices – access to information has become faster and easier than ever before. In today's environment, the information that Generation Alpha is exposed to has reached dimensions incomparable to the past. Therefore, besides having access to information and producing it, it has become important for Generation Alpha to be able to select and manage it as well. To this point, in the preparation of the educational environment, it is useful and necessary to get to know the people who are studying at school today, to learn the content and the skills that should be provided to them, to determine their needs and expectations, and to prepare them for the foreseeable future.

As is well known, today's educational system is based on 21st-century skills. Information literacy, statistical literacy, and data literacy are the bases of such 21st-century skills, which include critical thinking, problem-solving, and strategic thinking (Fontichiaro & Oehrli, 2016; Shields, 2005). Therefore, it is unquestionable that the generation born into the highest technology currently possible should have a learning environment designed for them based on these three skills.

A summary of these three skills suggested to be essential in the education of Generation Alpha is thus: information literacy, an individual's right to ask the right information and find the correct data source; statistical literacy, the ability of the individual to fully grasp the context behind the statistics presented to them in order to interpret them correctly; data literacy, the ability to collect, manage, evaluate, and use data in decision-making processes (Ridsdale et al., 2015; Carey, Grainger & Christie, 2018). In fact, data literacy is named by Chinien and Boutin (2011) as the essential survival skill of the 21st century.

Information literacy is defined at the most basic level as the ability to identify what information is needed, find it, and use it effectively (Shields, 2005; Carlson et al., 2011). From this perspective, information literacy is the key to the future of industrial societies (Harkins, 2008; Puncreobutr, 2016). However, in developing and using this major skill, a number of subordinate skill sets have to be developed and used.

As information has come to be summarized using statistics, information literacy has been replaced by statistical literacy (Fig. 1). Statistics can be defined as numerical expressions used to summarize information (Gould, 2017). The ability of an individual to understand, interpret, and evaluate the reality behind the statistics presented is statistical literacy (Shields, 2005). While these three skills are basically built on top of each other, there are differences in nuance between them. As can be understood from the above brief definitions and explanations, data literacy – different from information literacy and statistical literacy –enables the individual to also interpret and make predictions based upon the available data by moving beyond simple evaluation of the situation. In this sense, the line

Fig. 1: Worldcloud of Statistical Terms.

that separates data literacy, on the one hand, from information literacy and statistical literacy, on the other, is that it provides the opportunity to extrapolate to the future by taking snapshots of the current situation. Therefore, data literacy includes statistical literacy, such as reading tables and graphs, and also information literacy skills, such as obtaining and using the necessary information (Fontichiaro & Oehrli, 2016; Gould, 2017). As such, information literacy and statistical literacy skills need to be acquired in order to base data literacy skills on solid foundations.

Data Literacy Skills

Data literacy, which is defined as the ability to access, manage, evaluate, and apply decision-making processes and which itself forms the basis of the decision-making process (Ridsdale et al., 2015), can be examined for teachers under three categories with related skills in order to understand and be effective for Generation Alpha. These categories are awareness, decision-making, and dissemination. Awareness can be defined as the individual being able to set goals for own personal development in order to improve the skills appropriate to the needs of today's world. For teachers in order to determine these goals, they should be able to evaluate themselves well, comprehend the requirements of the period in which they live, and assess the areas in which they should develop by evaluating the former. Decision-making covers the basic statistical concepts, and

Awareness	Decision making	Dissemination
-Awares of the concept and characteristics of data literacy. -Awares of the qualities that an individual should have in the 21st century. -Sets goals for self-improvement.	-Has knowledge of basic statistical concepts. -Knows data types. -Chooses necessary data type/s to find answers to his/her questions. -Selects/creates a data source. -Manages the data collection process. -Determines the analysis method. -Runs the analysis process. -Edits and visualizes data. -Reads tables, charts, graphs.	-Evaluates analysis results. -Creates reports about analysis results. -Makes judgements based on analysis reports. -Makes decisions using solid results.

Tab. 1: Teacher's Data Literacy Skills

the selection and application of methods of analysis. Dissemination refers to the teacher making judgments by interpreting the results of the analysis and using data literacy skills in contexts, other than the learning experience (Means et al., 2009). Here the teacher is expected to be able to transfer data literacy skills into real world practice or the professional development process. Teacher's data literacy skills under these three categories are presented in Tab. 1.

Awareness

In the process of acquiring data literacy skills, it is important for a teacher to recognize this skill and to identify their own deficiencies. Under this category, a teacher is expected to be knowledgeable about the skills involved in information literacy, statistical literacy, and data literacy. In addition, a teacher should be aware of what competencies they should have within the framework of the needs of Generation Alpha, as well as the areas in which they need to be developed. Awareness is a category covering some data literacy skills which are explained as follows;

Knowledge of the concept of literacy and its characteristics includes knowledge about the various definitions and types of literacy. It is expected that an individual will be able to express what qualities they need in order to be literate. From this point of view, an understanding of the basic concepts and terminology of literacy is essential. For example, Kurudayıoğlu and Tüzel (2010) understand the definition of literacy as more than just literacy, examining the concept under the four sub-categories of media literacy, information literacy, electronic literacy, and mother language literacy. Further, they maintain that there are separate skills implicit in each type of literacy. As can be seen here, being aware of other literacy types as well as data literacy, and possessing those skills, will enable the teacher to be proficient in data literacy.

In the 21st century, the individual is expected to know, by considering the needs and problems of today's world, what abilities are required of the labor force. Therefore, it is important that a teacher be able to analyze the needs of society by closely following the changing and developing world. In the Knowledge Synthesis Report published by Dalhouse University in 2015, critical thinking, problem-solving, and computational thinking are among the 21st-century skills. However, it was stated that these skills cannot be directly integrated into the existing curriculum systems. In addition, the same report holds that critical thinking is the foundational skill in data literacy. This is because it is essential to ask the right questions and examine the results with a critical eye while working with data. Problem-solving requires careful observation of the area you are in while looking for necessary data to collect in order to solve a problem using optimum resources and the best way. Combining these two skills, computational thinking requires equal measures of both critical thinking and problem-solving skills.

Awareness also covers the ability to set goals for self-improvement, and it can be defined as the ability of the individual to determine, within the framework of 21st-century skills and the qualifications required of the workforce, one's own literacy level and needs for self-improvement. Within the scope of this skill, a teacher should do self-evaluation objectively, taking into consideration own existing knowledge, and set achievable goals. The teacher will thus be motivated throughout the process. In doing so, a teacher needs to make a multilateral assessment trying to find answer to these questions; Which of the 21st-century skills do I possess? Which should I improve? What are the capabilities expected of a qualified workforce? Which of these qualities should I have or develop? As a result of such an evaluation of qualifications and competencies, teachers have to create a roadmap by identifying the gap between what they have and what they lack to determine what they need to do in order to cover the difference between the two.

Decision-Making

Teachers are generally expected to have basic statistical literacy skills. Knowledge of basic statistical concepts implies that the teacher is expected to have mastery of statistical terms and terminology at a conceptual level and to know the equivalent of these terms in practice. This skill is particularly important as it provides the basis for other skills within data literacy. Knowledge of basic statistical concepts is analogous to knowing the alphabet of data literacy. We can say that such proficiency is thus the basic skill for being data literate.

Knowledge of data types implies the ability to determine the level of measurement of the available data, which the teacher achieves using knowledge about subjects such as measurement levels and scale types. Additionally, a teacher with this skill should be able to list the differences between the data types. With this ability, the teacher is able to determine which type of data fits with what kind of question, and to extrapolate from the relevant data type to the determination of which inferences can be asked to answer a variety of different questions.

The ability to select and create a data source corresponds to where or from whom teachers can obtain data, in cases where the teacher needs data other than the data presented to them. A teacher with this skill should be able to give examples of different data sources. For example, they should be able to obtain data from social media, a written text, or video. Furthermore, should be able to choose not only the data themselves but also the data source correctly. Selecting or creating a data source that is not suitable for the target data may lead to data acquisition outside the scope of purpose, which may play a distracting role and slow the data collection process down from reaching its intended target.

The ability to manage the data collection process is related to that process being fully controlled in a systematic, intertwined process, which requires careful monitoring in order for the individual to access healthy data from the right source. In this context, a teacher should determine the data source correctly, conduct the process ethically without error, and monitor the data continuously. First of all, teachers should reach the correct data source and follow the necessary protocols for the data collection process and proceed according to the plan they made previously. In this respect, it is very important for teachers to be conscious of the importance of data-based studies.

The ability to determine the method of analysis actually refers to a multi-step process by which an individual examines the data, determines a method of analysis appropriate to the structure of the data set, and arranges the data to perform this analysis. A method that is not appropriate to the data set often leads the individual to false inferences, and in some cases may not lead to any conclusions at all. The method of interpreting the data set is equally important for the accuracy of the data set. Therefore, teachers must be able to perform all the behaviors of all the skills dealt with up to this point.

After determining the method of analysis, the ability to perform the analysis is, simply, the ability of teachers to follow the method of analysis step by step in accordance with the data. In this process, the individual must follow the relevant procedure for analysis through to completion.

Data editing and table reading skills include behaviors such as cleaning and editing the data set by examining the data. A teacher should identify any abnormalities or errors in the data set. This cleared data set should then be arranged in a meaningful way, without loss of data, to explain the current situation. When examining the table, it is possible to see which parts are correct and which parts are wrong and that they can intervene without disturbing the data. At the same time, a teacher should be able to prepare multiple tables of the same data set. For this reason, a teacher must be familiar with different tabulation operations, the shape of the table, columns, rows, and so on. In addition, a teacher is expected to be able to read and explain the situation both prepared by himself and one presented to him. One of the ways to improve this data editing and table reading skill set is to make explanations and interpretations of different tables prepared with the same data, if possible, at the difficulty level appropriate to the target audience. Another option is to read and interpret data via providing tables that include the things they would like to learn, containing topics that align with the interests of individuals.

Data visualization refers to the individual's ability to determine and create the correct graph type in order to express the presented data visually in a meaningful way (Wang, Wang & Alexander, 2015) A teacher should be able to put together and present multiple images in order to explain the data set. In addition, a teacher should be able to explain the current situation by reading and interpreting a data image presented to them. A teacher should be able to reach a judgment, especially by reading and understanding different types of graphics. Data visualization is an easy way to see and understand trends, outliers, and patterns in data, using visual elements such as tables, graphs, and maps. With the advancement of developing technology and computer science, these visuals are not only presented with tables and graphics, but also with infographics, three-dimensional visuals, histograms, and even interactive visuals. When choosing from among these image options, it is important to determine the visualization method that will convey the data in the most accurate way for target learners. For example, when working with various data, it would be more meaningful to present a three-dimensional image using various computer programs rather than, say, a table. As another example, we can use an infographic (e.g. Fig. 2.) to explain steps in a process or a timeline to display the transfer of data obtained over a long period of time.

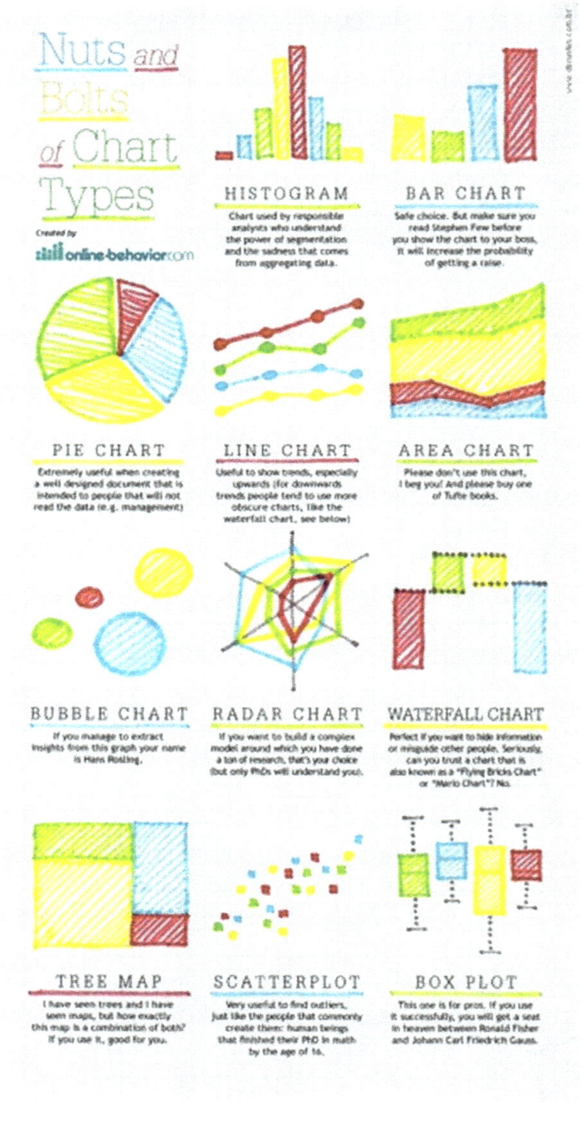

Fig. 2: Chart & Graph Types Infographic (Waisberg, 2011)

Dissemination

The ability to evaluate the result of the analysis refers to the interpretation and evaluation of the individual's completed analysis. For this skill, a teacher is expected to convert statistical knowledge into practice.

Similar to others, creating reports about analysis results requires other subskills and information like statistic literacy, knowing data types, creating tables, etc. for a teacher. Creating reports about analysis reports is also important both to see specific points and get overall idea and share these results with administration, parents, or learners personally.

The ability to make a judgment based on the result of the analysis is just that – a teacher's judgment made by interpreting the results of the analysis which is also connected with other data literacy skills because the form of results may change depending on the data analysis tool or technique.

By making proper judgments an individual becomes capable of making right decisions using solid results. It enables a teacher to create personalized plans for students individually or more generally making tailor-made lesson plans for specific purposes.

Closing Remarks

Although there have been many years of educational studies on various types of literacy, the skills specific to these genres, and the areas in which they interact, educational innovations are currently needed, as change, in terms of the readiness of the students as well as the innovations in every field, is increasingly the norm. The members of Generation Alpha, who are presumed to be particularly capable of rapidly adapting to technology and all innovations presented by technology may occasionally fail to make sense of the statistics presented to them or to visualize the data they face in real life (Fontichiaro & Oehrli, 2016). On the other hand, from the perspective that data literacy is one of the most fundamental skills operant in providing products and services customizable to the usage habits and needs of individuals, product or service providers should also acquire data literacy skills, especially given that Generation Alpha tends to prefer personalized products and services (Roberts, Newman, & Schwartzstein, 2012). In other words, it is even more important for teachers who are designing learning environments for Generation Alpha to possess data literacy skills.

There are many reasons why data literacy, the basic life skill of the 21st century, is becoming increasingly important. But perhaps what makes this skill so important is that data is critical to produce an effective policy, persuading others, developing strong arguments, and developing effective strategies (Barlow, 2015). Therefore, for those aiming to become the leading country of tomorrow, the primary focus of managers should be to provide Generation Alpha with data literacy skills.

References

Barlow, D. (2015). The basics of data literacy: Helping your students (and you!) make sense of data. *The Education Digest*, *80*(7), 61.

Carey, M., Grainger, P., & Christie, M. (2018). Preparing preservice teachers to be data literate: A Queensland case study. *Asia-Pacific Journal of Teacher Education*, *46*(3), 267–278.

Carlson, J., Fosmire, M., Miller, C., & Nelson, M. S. (2011). Determining data information literacy needs: A study of students and research faculty. *Portal: Libraries and the Academy*, *11*(2), 629–657.

Chinien, C., & Boutin, F. (2011). *Defining essential digital skills in the Canadian workplace*: Human Resources and Skills Development Canada.

Fontichiaro, K., & Oehrli, J. A. (2016). Why data literacy matters. *Knowledge Quest*, *44*(5), 21–27.

Gould, R. (2017). Data literacy is statistical literacy. *Statistics Education Research Journal*, *16*(1), 22–25.

Harkins, A. M. (2008). Leapfrog principles and practices: Core components of education 3.0 and 4.0. *Futures Research Quarterly*, *24*(1), 19–31.

Kurudayıoğlu, M., & Tüzel, S. (2010). 21. yüzyıl okuryazarlık türleri, değişen metin algısı ve Türkçe eğitimi. *Türklük Bilimi Araştırmaları,* (28), 283–298.

Means, B., Padilla, C., DeBarger, A., & Bakia, M. (2009). *Implementing data-informed decision making in schools: Teacher access, supports and use*. US Department of Education. Retrieved from: https://files.eric.ed.gov/fulltext/ED504191.pdf

Puncreobutr, V. (2016). Education 4.0: New challenge of learning. *St. Theresa Journal of Humanities and Social Sciences*, *2*(2), 92–97.

Ridsdale, C., Rothwell, J., Smit, M., Ali-Hassan, H., Bliemel, M., Irvine, D., . . . Wuetherick, B. (2015). Strategies and best practices for data literacy education: Knowledge synthesis report.

Roberts, D. H., Newman, L. R., & Schwartzstein, R. M. (2012). Twelve tips for facilitating Millennials' learning. *Medical Teacher*, *34*(4), 274–278.

Shields, M. (2005). Information literacy, statistical literacy, data literacy. *IASSIST Quarterly*, *28*(2–3), 6–6.

Waisberg, D. (2011). Nuts and Bolts of Chart & Graph Types [infographic]. Retrieved August 20, 2019, from https://online-behavior.com/analytics/chart-types

Wang, L., Wang, G., & Alexander, C. A. (2015). Big data and visualization: methods, challenges and technology progress. *Digital Technologies*, *1*(1), 33–38.

List of Figures

List of Tables

About the Editor

Nihal Yurtseven, PhD, is an assistant professor at the Department of Educational Sciences, Bahçeşehir University, Istanbul, Turkey. She received her PhD degree in curriculum and instruction with a specialization in instructional design at Yildiz Technical University, Istanbul, Turkey. So far, she has researched about instructional design, teachers' professional development, the relationship between teachers' professional development and students' achievement, and numerous variables affecting student learning. Specifically, she has carried out several experimental, mixed method, and action research studies to understand the impact of instructional interventions on the learning process. In addition, she has organized seminars and workshops about the integration of instructional design models into diverse disciplines at various educational institutions, and she has presented her studies in different conferences. Teacher education, instructional design, mentorship, teamwork, professional learning communities, peer coaching, and individual differences are among her fields of interest. She has various scientific studies, book chapters, and national/international presentations about these fields. She also has been teaching courses in the field of educational sciences at graduate and undergraduate level. She is currently the coordinator of a national project, named Designer Teacher.
E-mail: nihal.yurtseven@es.bau.edu.tr

About the Authors

Şirin Karadeniz, PhD, is a full professor at Bahçeşehir University. She received her Bachelor's degree in Computer Systems Education, Master's degree in Computer Education and doctorate degree in Educational Technology. She has given undergraduate and postgraduate courses in the fields of integration of innovative technologies to education, coding and robotics teaching, and STEM. In addition, she has carried out trainings, seminars, and workshops to stakeholders at national and international level in the mentioned fields. She also carried out projects with the relevant ministries and international organizations as well as non-governmental organizations. In 2016, she received the Successful Woman Educator of the Year Award in Women Leaders of Technology competition, organized in the partnership of Microsoft and Kagider. In 2018, she was awarded with BAU Social Benefit Award for her contribution to education. She has worked as a coordinator, researcher, expert, and consultant in national and international projects in TUBITAK, MONE, UNICEF, World Bank, and European Union. Dr. Karadeniz has published national books, national and international book chapters, articles, and papers in the field of educational technology. Dr. Karadeniz currently serves as the President of Bahçeşehir University. E-mail: sirin.karadeniz@bau.edu.tr

Ahmet Aydemir, PhD, is a psychologist, sociologist, and organizational behaviorist who works as the director of the International Training Center for Authorities and Leaders, CIFAL Istanbul, an affiliated training center of the United Nations Institute for Training and Research (UNITAR), an institution focused on educating the world to achieve the United Nations Sustainable Development Goals (UN SDGs). He is an instructor at the Faculty of Educational Sciences at Bahçeşehir University, and a member of the Turkish Psychologists Association (TPD), American Psychological Association (APA), American Sociological Association (ASA), and People Management Association of Turkey (PERYÖN). E-mail: ahmet.aydemir@es.bau.edu.tr

Enisa Mede, PhD, is Associate Professor at the Department of English Language Teaching (ELT) of Bahçeşehir University, Istanbul, Turkey. She has been in the academia for 10 years. Her research interests lie in the area of program design and evaluation in second/foreign language education, bilingual education, and first/second language development in young learners. She has authored numerous articles in indexed journals and book chapters. She has been offering Teaching

Language Skills, Young Learners, School Experience, and Practicum courses at the undergraduate level and Curriculum Development in Language Education, Syllabus Design and Evaluation, and Second Language Acquisition courses at the graduate level. E-mail: enisa.mede@es.bau.edu.tr

Ayşin Kaplan Sayı, PhD, is an assistant professor at the Department of Gifted and Talented Education postgraduate program, Bahçeşehir University, Istanbul. She received her PhD in Gifted and Talented education with a specialization of differentiated instruction, critical thinking, and creativity. She has been designing educational programs, and she organizes university camps for gifted children since 2005. She has created projects for cultivating gifted education in Turkey, and she has articles on gifted and talented education, differentiation, critical thinking, and creativity. E-mail: aysin.kaplansayi@es.bau.edu.tr

Sabiha Dulay, PhD, is an assistant professor at the Department of Educational Administration and Planning, Bahçeşehir University. She completed her undergraduate degree (2007–2011) in English Language Teaching at Dokuz Eylül University, her MA (2011–2013), and PhD (2013–2017) in Educational Administration, Inspection, Planning and Economics at Eskisehir Osmangazi University. She has been teaching courses such as Introduction to Educational Sciences, Research Methods at undergraduate level, and Conflict Management, Organizational Behavior and Leadership, and Education Systems in the World at graduate level. Dr. Dulay has national and international publications on leadership, organizational commitment, organizational climate, teacher typologies in classroom management, school principals as socials actors, and educational policies. Email: sabiha.dulay@es.bau.edu.tr

Gürsu Aşık, PhD, received his integrated BS and MS degree from Secondary School Science and Mathematics Education at Boğaziçi University in 2006. He pursued his MS studies in the same department and graduated in 2009. Meanwhile, he began to work as a research assistant in the Department of Primary Education. He received his PhD degree in mathematics education from Marmara University in 2015 and started to work as a full-time faculty member in the Faculty of Educational Sciences at Bahçeşehir University. At the same time, he continues to work as a measurement and evaluation coordinator at the Center for Learning and Teaching (CLT) in the same university. Dr. Aşık's academic research interests predominantly focus on teaching mathematics and measurement and evaluation. More specifically, he is interested in students' metacognitive regulations, problem-solving skills, raising and maintaining students' curiosity in learning and teaching. Email: gursu.asik@es.bau.edu.tr

Hülya Avci is currently a new doctoral student in Learning Design and Technology in the Department of Educational Psychology at Texas A&M University. She has an MA degree in Educational Technology at Bahçeşehir University and a BA degree in Foreign Languages Education at Yildiz Technical University, Istanbul, Turkey. She worked as an EFL instructor for six years at a foundation university in Istanbul. Her research interests include learning technologies, instructional design, problem-based learning, and game-based learning. Email: hulya.avci@email.tamu.edu

Tufan Adıgüzel, PhD, is a full professor at the Department of Computer Education and Instructional Technologies, Bahçeşehir University, Istanbul. He was also a founder and a coordinator of Distance Education and STEM Units. He received his PhD in educational psychology with a specialization in educational technology at Texas A&M University, where he was a member of the Data to Knowledge (D2K) research team studying technologies for science education of students with disabilities. He has been teaching courses such as "Instructional Design," "Multimedia Design and Production," and "Distance Education" at undergraduate and graduate levels. With more than 23 years of corporate and academic experience in "Educational Technology," Dr. Adıgüzel has numerous national and international projects and publications on technology integration into math, science and special education and adaptive technologies. E-mail: tufan.adiguzel@es.bau.edu.tr

Ergün Akgün, PhD, graduated from Muğla University Primary School Teaching Department in 2007. He received his master's degree from Hacettepe University, Institute of Science and Technology in Computer Education and Instructional Technology in 2012. He completed his PhD at Dumlupınar University on the estimation of student achievement with artificial neural networks in 2017. He worked as a research assistant at Uşak University Faculty of Education between 2008 and 2018. His research areas are classroom teaching, distance education, educational data mining, educational use of artificial intelligence, and classification analysis. He is currently a faculty member of Bahçeşehir University Faculty of Educational Sciences and the director of Office of Distance Education Unit at Bahçeşehir University. E-mail: ergun.akgun@de.bau.edu.tr

www.ingramcontent.com/pod-product-compliance
Ingram Content Group UK Ltd.
Pitfield, Milton Keynes, MK11 3LW, UK
UKHW022222051026
15624UKWH00002B/308

9 783631 809778